PAT BROWN, MBA

Financial Literacy For Engineers

"The Engineer's Playbook for Budgeting, Investing, and Financial Freedom"

ABRAM · 47 · BROWN

First published by AbramBrown47 2025

First edition

ISBN: 978-1-967737-24-6

This book was professionally typeset on Reedsy.
Find out more at reedsy.com

Contents

Preface

Why Engineers Need Financial Literacy—Now More Than Ever

Engineers are some of the smartest, most skilled professionals in the world. You solve complex problems, build systems from scratch, and approach challenges with logic, discipline, and precision. But when it comes to money—budgeting, investing, taxes, insurance, debt—many engineers feel underprepared.

It's not a lack of intelligence. It's a lack of information.

Most engineers never received formal financial education in school. You were taught how to design machines, write code, analyze data, and optimize systems—but not how to read a paycheck, make a retirement plan, or build long-term wealth. And as your income grows, so does the complexity of your financial life.

The result? Too many engineers make great money… but feel stuck, confused, or behind financially. Some are overwhelmed by student loans. Others wait too long to start investing. Many overthink every decision or avoid it altogether—paralyzed by perfectionism, unsure who to trust, and afraid to make a mistake.

That's where this book comes in.

I wrote *Financial Literacy For Engineers* because I believe engineers deserve better. You deserve financial guidance that respects your intelligence, speaks your language, and helps you use your skills not just at work—but in your life.

As a financial literacy advocate with over two decades of experience,

I've worked with engineers across all fields—software, civil, mechanical, electrical, aerospace—and I've seen a common pattern: when you finally learn how to manage money like you manage projects, everything changes. Your stress decreases. Your confidence grows. Your future opens up.

This book won't teach you how to get rich overnight. But it will show you how to build financial strength step by step—using the same strategic thinking that makes you successful in your career.

Money doesn't have to be confusing.

Financial planning doesn't have to be overwhelming.

You just need the right framework—and that starts here.

Let's build something strong, smart, and sustainable.

Let's build your financial future.

— Pat Brown, MBA

Financial Literacy Advocate & Wealth Advisor

Author of Financial Literacy For Engineers

Why Financial Literacy for Engineers Matters

Engineers are trained to solve the world's toughest problems—but too often, their own financial life remains a mystery.

You can model systems, debug code, design machinery, or build infrastructure that supports entire cities. But when it comes to managing money—budgeting, investing, retirement planning, or navigating taxes—many engineers find themselves operating without a blueprint.

This isn't a knock on engineers.

It's a reflection of a broader truth: **most highly educated professionals were never taught how money really works.**

Financial literacy isn't built into engineering school curriculums. There's no "Money 101" course in most undergraduate programs, no financial literacy module in graduate studies, and no real-world training on how to navigate the wealth-building process.

As a result, many engineers:

- **Earn great incomes but still live paycheck to paycheck**
- **Delay investing out of fear of making a mistake**
- **Overanalyze every money decision and experience "financial paralysis"**
- **Ignore taxes and insurance until it's too late**
- **Avoid working with advisors because they don't trust someone "outside the numbers"**

Here's the irony: engineers are perfectly equipped to excel financially.

You already understand systems, optimization, trade-offs, data, and compound results. Those same principles apply to money.

- Budgeting is a resource allocation problem.
- Investing is a long-term risk/reward equation.
- Retirement planning is a systems design challenge with constraints and inputs.
- Taxes are a series of if/then logic problems.
- Insurance is about probability, impact, and risk mitigation.

When you think of your financial life like a system—something you can model, test, and improve—it becomes far more manageable. You don't need to know everything. You just need to know how to think about it like an engineer.

What's at Stake

Without financial literacy, even brilliant engineers can end up:

- Trapped in jobs they no longer enjoy because of financial obligations
- Paying unnecessary interest, fees, or penalties due to poor planning
- Missing out on early investment opportunities that could compound for decades
- Lacking the confidence to negotiate better salaries, stock options, or contracts
- Entering retirement unprepared—despite earning six figures for years

And that's not just bad for individuals—it's bad for families, communities, and industries that depend on financially secure professionals.

What's Possible

With financial literacy, engineers can:

- Build wealth confidently and systematically
- Align their income with their values and long-term goals
- Gain the freedom to take career risks, start businesses, or retire early
- Protect their families and plan legacies
- Model smart financial behavior for the next generation

Engineers don't need more financial hype. You need clear, honest, data-driven guidance.

This book exists to give you exactly that.

Because when engineers master their money, they don't just build wealth—they build freedom, security, and a legacy of smart decision-making.

And in a world full of uncertainty, that matters more than ever.

My Personal Mission to Help Engineers Build Wealth

I didn't start my career as an engineer. But I've spent more than two decades working alongside them—as a financial advisor, educator, and advocate for financial literacy. And over the years, I've noticed a frustrating pattern:

Engineers are some of the most capable, disciplined, and intelligent professionals I've ever met—yet they're often underprepared when it comes to money.

That disconnect stuck with me.

It wasn't because engineers were careless. It was because the financial world often speaks a language that doesn't match how engineers think. It's filled with vague advice, emotional pitches, and overly simplified rules of thumb. There's too much noise, and not enough clarity.

Meanwhile, engineers are looking for logic. For systems. For structure. For something that actually *works.*

That's why I made it my mission to bridge that gap.

I Believe This:

- **Engineers deserve financial education that matches their mindset.**
- Not fluff. Not fear. Just smart frameworks, real math, and practical tools.
- **You shouldn't have to figure it all out on your own.**
- You weren't taught this in school—and most financial "advice" out there either talks down to you or talks around you.

- **The better engineers do with money, the more impact they can have.**
- On their families. On their communities. On the world. I've seen too many people with great technical talent trapped by financial stress—and too many with real freedom using it to create something bigger than themselves.

That's why this book exists.

This is more than just a career for me. It's a calling. I believe financial literacy is the foundation for freedom, purpose, and legacy. I believe it's a right—not a luxury. And I believe engineers are uniquely positioned to thrive once they're given the right tools.

If this book helps even one engineer feel more confident, more free, and more in control of their financial future, it's worth every page.

I'm honored to walk this journey with you.

Let's build wealth—on purpose, with precision, and for the long run.

— Pat Brown, MBA

Financial Literacy Advocate

How to Approach This Book Like an Engineer

Engineers don't wing it. You're trained to think critically, test variables, and build systems that work under pressure. The same mindset that makes you great at engineering can be your biggest asset in building wealth—**if you apply it intentionally.**

This book is not about hype or hope. It's about **systems**, **strategy**, and **sustainability**.

It's about treating your financial life the same way you would approach a technical challenge:

1. Start with a Clear Objective

In engineering, you define the end goal before building.

Your financial life is no different.

Are you trying to become debt-free? Retire early? Build generational wealth? Start your own firm?

Begin by identifying your financial "specs." What does success look like for you?

This will shape the way you move through this book and implement what you learn.

2. Respect the System Interactions

Your finances are not isolated components—they're an interconnected system.

Budgeting, debt, investing, insurance, taxes, and income all affect one another.

Change one, and you may impact the others.

This book is designed with that systems thinking in mind.

You'll see how each financial decision has second- and third-order consequences—just like in your designs.

3. Don't Wait for Perfect—Iterate

Many engineers are perfectionists. You want the best answer, the most optimized solution, the cleanest code.

But money doesn't work that way. You'll never have all the variables known at once.

Instead, take a prototype approach:

- Start with a simple budget
- Begin investing even if you're not 100% sure
- Review, revise, and improve over time

Iterate like you would in product development: progress > perfection.

4. Automate What Can Be Automated

Engineers love efficiency—and your money should be efficient, too.

Automate:

- Savings contributions
- Investment allocations
- Bill payments

- Debt paydowns

Set up systems once and let them run with minimal oversight, just like a well-coded control loop.

5. Use Data and Logic—But Trust Your Values

Yes, data matters. Yes, logic matters. But your money should also reflect your **values**, not just cold math.

- Do you want more time with family?
- Do you care about giving back?
- Do you dream of freedom, not just more?

The numbers are your tools. But your *why* is your blueprint.

6. Monitor and Maintain Like a Professional

A bridge doesn't last 100 years without inspections.

Neither does a financial plan.

Revisit your numbers monthly. Rebalance investments annually. Check your financial "structural integrity" often.

Routine maintenance is boring—but it keeps everything from collapsing later.

7. Know When to Call in Experts

You don't design a skyscraper without consulting architects, safety engineers, or code experts.

Similarly, you don't have to do everything in your financial life alone.

Knowing when to work with a:

- **Financial advisor**

- **CPA**
- **Estate planning attorney**
- **Insurance professional**

...is part of being a smart engineer. It's not a sign of weakness—it's a sign of strategic thinking.

In Short:

- Think in systems
- Start with your specs
- Iterate and automate
- Balance logic with values
- Maintain your plan
- Use experts when needed

Approach your financial life like the biggest, most meaningful project you'll ever build—because it is.

This time, **you're the client, the designer, the architect, and the engineer** all rolled into one.

So let's build a life that works—for now, and for decades to come.

Part I: Mindset Engineering – Building Your Financial Framework

Before you start budgeting, investing, or optimizing your taxes, you need the right operating system—your mindset.

Part I lays the foundation for everything that follows. This section challenges the way engineers traditionally think about money and reframes financial literacy through a systems lens. You'll explore how to apply core engineering principles—like systems thinking, iterative design, and root cause analysis—to your personal finances.

Engineers thrive on data, logic, and structure, but when it comes to money, many are left without a roadmap. In these chapters, you'll learn how to treat your financial life as a complex, evolving system that you can model, test, and improve over time. You'll also confront common psychological and emotional barriers that hold high-performing professionals back—like perfectionism, over-analysis, or fear of making financial mistakes.

This part of the book will help you shift from reactive to proactive thinking. You'll learn to define your financial goals clearly, assess your relationship with money honestly, and recognize how your decision-making style affects long-term wealth building.

Whether you're just starting your career or already earning six figures, this section will give you the mental framework to approach money with confidence, control, and clarity.

By the end of Part I, you won't just be ready to make smart financial decisions—you'll be ready to think like an engineer *about* money.

Chapter 1: Systems Thinking Applied to Money

Most engineers understand the power of a well-designed system. Whether you're managing a supply chain, writing code for an app, or analyzing structural integrity, you rely on interconnected components working together toward a desired outcome. Your financial life should be no different.

In this chapter, we'll explore how to apply systems thinking to money. Not just as a metaphor—but as a practical, actionable approach to building financial stability and long-term wealth.

The Engineer's Edge: Thinking in Systems

Systems thinking is what separates reactive problem-solving from proactive strategy. It's the difference between patching a leak and redesigning the pipeline.

When you treat your finances like a system:

- You identify core components (income, expenses, debt, savings, investments, insurance)
- You understand their interactions and dependencies
- You create feedback loops, automation, and redundancies
- You can model outcomes, test decisions, and refine over time

Just like you wouldn't isolate a design component from the larger assembly, you can't make good money decisions in a vacuum.

Step One: Define the Output (What Does Success Look Like?)

Every system starts with an objective. So ask yourself:

- What does financial success mean to me?
- What are the key performance indicators (KPIs) for my financial life?
- What timeline am I working with?

This may be early retirement, funding your kids' college, becoming debt-free, or achieving financial independence by a certain age. Your definition drives the rest of your system design.

Step Two: Map the System Components

Let's break down your personal financial system:

- **Inputs**: Salary, side hustle income, bonuses, investment returns
- **Processes**: Budgeting, investing, saving, debt repayment, tax strategy
- **Outputs**: Net worth, cash flow surplus, reduced liabilities, wealth growth
- **Feedback Loops**: Monthly budget reviews, portfolio rebalancing, tax withholding checks

Visualizing your finances as an interconnected flowchart can reveal inefficiencies and opportunities. Tools like spreadsheets, net worth trackers, and budgeting apps help you simulate and monitor your system.

Step Three: Identify Constraints and Trade-Offs

Every engineer knows that constraints define a system. In personal finance, your constraints might be:

- Income ceilings (for now)
- Fixed expenses (rent, loans)
- Risk tolerance
- Time (years to retirement)

And your trade-offs may include:

- Paying off student debt vs. investing in a Roth IRA
- Buying vs. renting
- Spending today vs. saving for tomorrow

Model these trade-offs like you would in a design spec. Run scenarios. Evaluate outcomes. Make decisions that reflect both logic and your life priorities.

Step Four: Optimize the Flow (Cash Flow Management)

Cash flow is the lifeblood of your system. You can make $200K/year and still feel broke if your system leaks.

To optimize:

- Automate savings and investments
- Route income into high-interest accounts
- Identify bottlenecks (subscriptions, lifestyle creep)
- Reduce financial drag (fees, interest payments)

Think of this like pressure loss in a piping system—reduce turbulence, friction, and leaks.

Step Five: Build in Redundancy and Risk Mitigation

Resilient systems have backups. So should your finances.

- Emergency fund = system redundancy
- Insurance = risk buffer
- Diversified investments = performance under varied conditions
- Estate plan = fail-safes for dependents

What happens if your income stops? What if you get hurt? What if markets crash? You don't need to predict the future—you just need to build a system that can absorb impact.

Real-World Scenarios

Scenario 1: A 24-year-old software engineer gets a $10,000 signing bonus. They're tempted to spend it all on a new gaming setup. But using systems thinking, they break the money down:

- $3,000 to emergency fund (redundancy)
- $2,000 to student loans (constraint relief)
- $3,000 to Roth IRA (long-term output)
- $2,000 for lifestyle (flexibility)

Scenario 2: A 45-year-old engineer realizes their net worth has stagnated. They trace it back to high cash drag—no automation, no investment plan, and growing discretionary expenses. They redesign their system: install auto-transfers to a brokerage account, cancel unused services, and set quarterly reviews.

Scenario 3: A 60-year-old mechanical engineer wants to retire in five years. They model various income sources (401(k), pension, Social Security) and design a drawdown plan with minimal tax impact and adequate liquidity.

Pros and Cons of Systems Thinking Applied to Money

Pros:

- Clear structure to make decisions
- Reduces emotional bias
- Enables long-term planning
- Creates consistency and efficiency

Cons:

- Can lead to over-analysis and decision delay
- Doesn't always account for emotional or relational financial decisions
- Requires active monitoring (though this can be reduced over time)

Action Steps

1. Sketch your financial system: income, expenses, assets, debts, savings, insurance.
2. Set your KPIs: monthly savings rate, debt reduction goals, net worth benchmarks.
3. Automate one process this week (e.g., transfer to savings).
4. Identify one constraint you can improve this month.
5. Schedule a 30-minute monthly review to assess the system.

Plain Language Concepts

- **Compound interest** is like feedback in a closed-loop control system: it grows with each cycle.
- **Diversification** is like redundancy in engineering design: it reduces the chance of catastrophic failure.
- **Budgeting** is resource allocation under constraints—sound familiar?
- **Insurance** is your circuit breaker—rarely used, but essential when

overloaded.

A Moment of Encouragement

You're more capable than you think. You already understand complex systems, trade-offs, and optimization. Now it's time to apply that same thinking to your money.

You don't need to guess. You just need a system.

The Takeaway

The smartest engineers don't guess with money—they model it, monitor it, and improve it over time.

Let this be your approach too.

Don't treat your financial life as a series of one-off choices. Design it like the critical system it is—because it supports everything else you want to build.

Final Note

This isn't just about being good with money. It's about:

- Owning your financial systems
- Owning your future
- Owning your peace of mind

Whatever stage you're at—from first paycheck to final paycheck—this mindset will serve you.

Let's build your financial engine with intention, logic, and strength. And let's start now.

Chapter 2: Financial Literacy: The New Essential Engineering Skill

There was a time when engineers were told to focus only on the technical. You were trained to solve problems, design systems, optimize resources, and bring structure to complexity. Finances? That was for the business majors. But times have changed.

Today, financial literacy is no longer a luxury or a "nice to have." For engineers navigating six-figure salaries, variable compensation, stock options, increasing costs of living, and retirement planning, **financial literacy is now a core competency**. Just like CAD, coding, structural analysis, or process flow design—**this is a skill that needs to be mastered.**

Let's make the case clearly: If you don't understand your own money, someone else will make decisions with it—or for it.

The Blind Spot: Why Many Engineers Ignore Money Until It's Too Late

Engineers tend to pride themselves on logic. But when it comes to money, many fall into common traps:

- You focus only on saving, not investing
- You overanalyze and delay decisions
- You assume your technical skill will always protect your income
- You outsource decisions without fully understanding them

This creates a dangerous blind spot: **You build great things for others, but don't build wealth for yourself.**

It's not because you lack intelligence. It's because financial topics aren't framed in ways that respect your training and problem-solving style.

That ends here.

Why Financial Literacy Is an Engineering Skill

Let's break it down:

- **Budgeting is resource management**
- **Investing is systems optimization under uncertainty**
- **Insurance is risk modeling and protection planning**
- **Taxes are constraint-bound routing problems**
- **Estate planning is contingency design**

You've already mastered harder concepts in your career than anything you'll face in personal finance. Once you reframe the topic through your own lens, it becomes clear:

You already have the tools—you just need to apply them differently.

How Financial Literacy Empowers Your Career

Let's take a real-world look at how understanding your finances enhances your professional life:

- **You negotiate better**: Engineers with a financial foundation understand total compensation—base salary, RSUs, ESPPs, benefits—and can evaluate offers holistically.
- **You make cleaner decisions**: Should you stay salaried or start a consulting business? Do you take the promotion or move across the country? Financial literacy gives you clarity on affordability and opportunity cost.

- **You reduce financial stress**: Engineers already work under pressure. Money stress compounds that. A confident handle on your financial world improves performance and focus.
- **You plan proactively**: Rather than reacting to changes in income or markets, you begin planning for early retirement, sabbaticals, or family needs.

What Financial Literacy Looks Like in an Engineering Career

Let's walk through different career stages and how financial literacy plays a role.

At 24, just starting out:

- You know how to build a budget that reflects your income and student loan payments
- You begin investing in your 401(k) early—even if it's just a little
- You understand why automating savings beats manually doing it later

At 35, mid-career:

- You balance raising a family with growing your net worth
- You review insurance policies like a project risk register
- You realize that your time and energy are assets—so you delegate tasks to financial professionals when needed

At 45, experienced and earning well:

- You evaluate equity vs fixed income, real estate, and other vehicles
- You begin planning for college expenses, potential business ventures, or partial early retirement
- You analyze tax strategies not just for today, but for the next 10–20 years

At 60, nearing retirement:

- You project income sources with precision (pension, Social Security, investment withdrawals)
- You structure drawdowns to minimize taxes and maintain liquidity
- You reframe retirement not as an end point—but as a new project

Plain Language Breakdowns of Complex Concepts

Let's take a few examples and demystify them:

- **Marginal Tax Brackets**: These are like tiers in a pressure vessel—only the top layer is taxed at the highest rate. Your entire income isn't taxed at 35%.
- **Stock Options**: Think of RSUs like deferred compensation with vesting rules. ISOs have favorable tax treatment but come with AMT triggers. Always model the timelines.
- **Insurance**: Life insurance is your backup power supply. Term is cheap and simple. Whole life is complex and rarely the best solution for engineers who want flexibility.
- **Compounding**: Exponential growth that engineers often use in models also applies here. Waiting to invest costs you more than being slightly wrong.
- **Diversification**: Think of this as component redundancy in mission-critical design. One fails? Others compensate.

Pros and Cons of Treating Financial Literacy Like a Technical Skill

Pros:

- Logical, step-by-step framework
- Reduces emotion and bias
- Promotes optimization and efficiency
- Engineers are already good at analyzing risk and trade-offs

Cons:

- May lead to over-optimization or analysis paralysis
- May overlook emotional or family dynamics
- Engineers may underestimate the value of delegation to financial professionals

Real-World Examples

"You're a 27-year-old civil engineer making $90K and thinking about buying a house. A friend tells you to put 20% down. But your student loans are 6.8% interest. What's the real trade-off?"

"You've been promoted to a lead position. Your employer gives you RSUs. You have no idea how they're taxed or when they vest. What's your next step?"

"You're 42, saving for your kids' college and wondering if you should max out a 529 or pay down your mortgage faster. How do you model that decision?"

"You're 60, and you've always handled the finances. But you're worried your spouse doesn't understand the plan. What should you do to simplify and document everything?"

These are real questions. Financial literacy is what turns these from guesses into strategic decisions.

Action Steps

1. List every financial account you have. Understand what each one does.
2. Write down your top 3 financial goals for the next 5 years.
3. Automate your savings or retirement contributions.
4. Read one article on marginal tax rates and one on index investing.
5. Schedule a quarterly "financial review" just like you'd run a project post-mortem.

A Moment of Encouragement

You've already learned how to solve complex problems under pressure. You've mastered tools, code, hardware, formulas.

You are more than capable of mastering your financial life.

What you've lacked isn't intelligence—it's a framework. This book is that framework.

Takeaway

The smartest engineers treat financial literacy as a skill to learn, not a mystery to fear.

Money isn't random. It follows patterns, rules, systems—and just like every system you've worked with, it rewards those who plan, test, and optimize.

Final Note

This isn't just about wealth.

It's about:

- Clarity in your decisions
- Peace in your home

- Purpose in your work
- Freedom in your life

If you can manage a project, lead a team, write code, or solve equations—then you can absolutely master your money.

Let's keep going. Let's build it, together.

Chapter 3: Problem-Solving Your Financial Life

Engineers solve problems for a living. You work through constraints, identify inefficiencies, and deliver solutions. But when it comes to personal finances, many engineers freeze. Not because they aren't capable—but because the problems feel too abstract, too emotional, or too far outside the familiar logic of their profession.

This chapter is about reclaiming your problem-solving power—applying the same methodical mindset you use at work to your money. You don't need to be a financial planner. You just need a framework, a set of tools, and the confidence to take the first step.

Financial Problems Are Engineering Problems

When you think about it, most financial issues are simply **poorly defined engineering problems.**

- Too much spending? That's a resource misallocation issue.
- Confusion around investing? That's a data-filtering problem.
- No retirement plan? That's a long-range forecasting gap.
- Debt piling up? That's a high-load system under stress.
- Living paycheck to paycheck? That's a lack of buffer or design tolerance.

What you need isn't more hustle. You need a **diagnostic model** and a system to test solutions.

Step One: Define the Real Problem

Just like you wouldn't throw parts at a machine without understanding the fault, don't throw money at financial issues without diagnosing the root cause.

Ask:

- What is the pain point I'm experiencing?
- What part of my financial system is underperforming?
- Is this a spending issue, an income issue, or a structural gap (like insurance or estate planning)?

Example: "I make good money, but I never feel like I'm getting ahead." Diagnosis: You need to audit your cash flow system and net worth growth rate.

Another: "I'm saving, but I'm not sure if I'm investing right." Diagnosis: You need to review your risk profile, timeline, and asset allocation.

Step Two: Model Possible Solutions

In engineering, you don't implement a fix before modeling the outcome. In financial planning, this means:

- Running retirement projections
- Modeling different debt repayment strategies
- Comparing rent vs. buy scenarios
- Stress testing your emergency fund against job loss

Example: You're paying off student loans at 5.5% and also considering maxing out your Roth IRA. Model:

- What happens if you do only minimum loan payments and invest the rest?
- What if you pay the loans down aggressively and delay investing?
- What does your net worth look like under both in 5 years?

Don't guess. Model it.

Step Three: Simplify the Decision Tree

Engineers often overthink because they can see *every variable.*

While it's true that financial decisions can be complex, 80% of the results usually come from a few key choices:

- **Spend less than you earn**
- **Invest early and consistently**
- **Manage risk through insurance and emergency reserves**
- **Automate good behavior**
- **Review and iterate quarterly**

Focus on first-order principles. Complexity can be layered in after the system is stable.

Step Four: Run Tests and Monitor Results

Just like you would test load capacity, signal integrity, or mechanical tolerance—**you should test your financial plan.**

- Does your budget actually reflect your values?
- Are you hitting your savings goals?
- Did that refinance or insurance change yield expected results?

Use tools:

- Net worth trackers
- Budget apps
- Excel dashboards
- Personal finance software

What gets measured gets improved.

Step Five: Course Correct Without Shame

When a design fails or a system crashes, you don't waste time with guilt—you debug and improve.

Approach your finances the same way:

- Made a bad investment? Analyze the lesson.
- Overspent last month? Adjust your categories.
- Forgot to contribute to your Roth IRA? Automate it next time.

Don't let perfectionism stall your progress. **Your financial system is a living project, not a final exam.**

Real-World Engineering Financial Problems

Case 1: A 24-year-old electrical engineer is earning $80K but still feels broke at the end of every month. After auditing their spending, they realize lifestyle creep (food delivery, gadget purchases, travel) is consuming 30% of take-home pay. They redesign the budget into categories, automate savings, and use a prepaid card for discretionary spending.

Case 2: A 35-year-old structural engineer is investing 10% into their 401(k), but hasn't increased the percentage since they got married or had kids. They model future college costs and realize they need to either boost savings or plan for student loans. They begin contributing to a 529 plan monthly.

Case 3: A 45-year-old software engineer earns $200K with stock options.

They don't understand the tax implications. They meet with a CPA, structure their exercise strategy across tax years, and use proceeds to fund a backdoor Roth IRA.

Case 4: A 60-year-old engineer is five years from retirement. They've accumulated $1.3 million but have no distribution plan. After modeling withdrawals, they restructure their portfolio, reduce risk exposure, and align investments with projected drawdown needs.

Pros and Cons of Solving Money Like a Technical Problem

Pros:

- Clear diagnostic paths
- Rational decision-making
- Structured experimentation
- Focus on results and continuous improvement

Cons:

- May undervalue emotional and behavioral factors
- Can lead to "over-designing" your finances
- May delay simple decisions in pursuit of a perfect model

Action Steps

1. Write down your top 3 financial problems.
2. Diagnose the root issue for each.
3. Sketch 2–3 possible solutions using modeling or projections.
4. Choose one and implement it for 30 days.
5. Evaluate results and iterate.

Bonus: Meet with a CPA or financial advisor and run a decision tree together.

Plain Language Breakdowns

- **Compound interest**: Like a feedback loop that amplifies gains over time. Early input matters.
- **Inflation**: The silent stress load your future dollars carry—needs regular offsetting.
- **Stock diversification**: Like building redundancy into a mechanical system.
- **Credit utilization**: The load percentage on your available credit lines—keep it low for optimal function.

A Moment of Encouragement

You don't need to know everything to start solving.

Start where you are. Use the tools you trust. Apply what you know from your career to your life.

You're more capable than you think.

The Takeaway

The smartest engineers don't guess with money. They diagnose. They test. They improve.

And when things break—they fix them.

Apply that mindset to your financial life, and you'll be ahead of 90% of the population.

Final Note

This book isn't just about building a better budget or maximizing your 401(k).

It's about engineering a life that gives you:

- More peace

- More freedom
- More purpose

Whatever challenges you face—financial or otherwise—you already have the core skill to overcome them: problem-solving.

Let's put it to work.

Chapter 4: Critical Path Method for Wealth Building

Engineers are no strangers to the Critical Path Method (CPM). You've used it to manage projects, schedule operations, and sequence construction or software tasks to meet deadlines efficiently. What if you applied the same mindset to your finances?

Wealth building, at its core, is a lifelong project. And like any complex initiative, it has dependencies, bottlenecks, resource constraints, and milestones. Understanding your personal financial critical path can help you prioritize decisions that move the needle most—and identify the distractions that don't.

In this chapter, we'll reframe your financial life using the Critical Path Method, turning your long-term wealth-building goals into a clear, trackable, engineer-designed process.

What Is the Critical Path in Your Financial Life?

In traditional project management, the critical path represents the **longest sequence of dependent tasks** that determine the minimum time needed to complete the project. Any delay in a critical path task delays the whole timeline.

Now apply this logic to wealth building:

- What are the key milestones between you and financial independence?

- What tasks (or decisions) are dependent on each other?
- What will cause delay if not addressed?

This is not theoretical. You can literally map it.

For example:

1. Pay off high-interest debt
2. Build emergency fund
3. Max out 401(k)
4. Open and fund Roth IRA
5. Invest in brokerage account
6. Purchase rental property

Every step builds on the one before. You can't retire early without investing consistently. You can't invest consistently if you're buried in credit card debt. That debt becomes a bottleneck on your path.

The critical path helps you focus on **sequence** and **leverage**.

Step One: Define Your Financial End Goal (Project Completion)

This is your project's finish line. For many, it's financial independence—when work becomes optional.

Define it clearly:

- How much income do you want each year in retirement?
- At what age?
- What lifestyle do you envision?

Then reverse engineer:

- What total net worth do you need?
- What annual return do you expect on investments?

- How many years of saving and investing does that require?

This becomes your project completion spec.

Step Two: Identify Your Milestones

List the major financial tasks or milestones required to reach that goal:

- Pay off debt
- Build 6-month emergency fund
- Max out tax-advantaged accounts
- Reach $100K invested
- Reach $500K net worth
- Purchase a home or investment property
- Build passive income streams
- Create estate plan

These are your work breakdown structure (WBS).

Step Three: Determine Dependencies and Bottlenecks

Not all steps can be done in parallel.

- You can't max out your 401(k) if you're living paycheck to paycheck
- You can't invest in real estate without down payment savings
- You can't calculate a FIRE number without understanding your retirement lifestyle cost

Start drawing arrows. Identify what *must* happen before something else can. These dependencies form your personal financial critical path.

Also ask:

- Where do I feel stuck?

- What decisions do I keep delaying?
- What's causing drag or delay?

Every unresolved question is a pending task on your timeline.

Step Four: Estimate Durations and Impact

For each item, estimate:

- How long it will take
- How much money it requires
- What the opportunity cost is

Then ask: What's the **ROI per unit of time and effort**?
Example:

- Paying off a $5,000 credit card at 20% interest saves you $1,000 a year.
- Maxing out a Roth IRA at $6,500/year might yield $50K in tax-free income over 20 years.
- Spending 10 hours understanding your company's 401(k) match might get you $3,000 a year for free.

Use this data to **prioritize** your time and resources.

Step Five: Optimize and Restructure the Path

Look for ways to shorten your timeline:

- Can you increase income to accelerate savings?
- Can you consolidate or refinance debt?
- Can you automate savings to remove friction?
- Can you eliminate or defer low-impact tasks?

Some tasks might belong on a parallel path, not the critical one. Others might need to be broken into phases.

Treat it like an engineering problem:

- What sequence gets you to the goal fastest with least risk?
- What tools or professionals do you need?
- Where are the inefficiencies?

Real-World Examples

Example 1: A 24-year-old engineer wants to retire by 50. They estimate needing $1.5 million.

- They start by eliminating student loans in 3 years
- Build $20K emergency fund
- Max out 401(k) and Roth IRA
- Use bonuses to fund a brokerage account
- Buy duplex at 32, creating rental income
- Reach $750K net worth by 40
- Downshift work at 50, living off investments and rental cash flow

Each step is part of their critical path.

Example 2: A 35-year-old mechanical engineer is unsure about when to buy a home vs invest.

- They model both:
- Buy now with 5% down and no investments for 5 years
- Rent and invest aggressively with 20%+ returns expected over 10 years
- After modeling, they buy a duplex instead and rent one side
- It becomes both shelter and income

This decision alters their entire timeline.

Pros and Cons of Critical Path Thinking in Finance

Pros:

- Clarifies priorities
- Highlights bottlenecks
- Enables sequence and strategic delegation
- Encourages resource allocation and efficiency

Cons:

- May over-focus on structure, leaving out emotional or personal values
- Can lead to rigidity—real life isn't always sequential
- Engineers may ignore rest or joy chasing efficiency

Action Steps

1. Write out your financial end goal (age, amount, lifestyle)
2. List every financial milestone you need to hit to get there
3. Identify which depend on others (what must happen first?)
4. Estimate time, cost, and return on each
5. Draw your personal financial critical path
6. Revisit and update every 6–12 months

Plain Language Breakdowns

- **FIRE Number**: Your target net worth where investments generate enough income to cover your annual expenses.
- **Opportunity Cost**: What you give up by choosing one path (e.g., spending $5K vs investing $5K).
- **Parallel Path**: Tasks you can do at the same time (e.g., save for a car while investing in 401(k)).
- **Bottleneck**: A task or expense that blocks multiple outcomes.

A Moment of Encouragement

Your wealth journey doesn't need to be chaotic. It can be designed, optimized, and built with intention.

Just like the projects you lead at work, this one matters. Probably more than any other.

And you're more equipped than you realize.

The Takeaway

The smartest engineers use Critical Path thinking to compress timelines, reduce waste, and achieve meaningful results.

Apply that same mindset to your wealth, and you'll build faster, stronger, and with far less stress.

Final Note

This chapter isn't about getting rich quick. It's about:

- Understanding the sequence that creates lasting wealth
- Focusing your time on the tasks that matter most
- Cutting through financial noise to gain clarity

Whether you're just launching or midway through your career, mapping your personal wealth-building critical path will help you:

- Protect your progress
- Accelerate your milestones
- Build a life that reflects your values

And isn't that the real measure of success?

Let's keep going.

Chapter 5: How Engineers Overcomplicate (and Oversimplify) Money

Let's call it like it is.

Engineers are brilliant. Detail-oriented. Pattern-seeking. Process-loving. They're the ones you trust to keep planes in the air, bridges from collapsing, and software from crashing. But when it comes to money?

They sometimes get in their own way.

This chapter is about two extremes: **overcomplicating** and **oversimplifying** your financial life. Both are common traps for engineers. And both can quietly stall progress if you're not careful.

You don't need to be a financial wizard to win with money. You need clarity, structure, and enough humility to admit when your brain is doing *too much*—or *too little.*

Let's walk through the symptoms, the reasons, and the practical strategies to strike the right balance.

Why Engineers Overcomplicate Money

Overcomplicating is rooted in the very traits that make you a great engineer:

- You love precision.
- You seek the optimal answer.

- You think in systems and edge cases.
- You don't like unknown variables.
- You don't want to make a mistake.

But here's the truth: **personal finance isn't a lab experiment.** You won't get perfect data. The goal isn't perfection—it's momentum.

Overcomplication shows up like this:

- Spending hours comparing ETFs with 0.03% vs 0.04% expense ratios
- Avoiding investing until you've read 10 books
- Building spreadsheets with 50 tabs but never setting up auto-transfers
- Waiting to contribute to your Roth IRA until you can "maximize the tax advantage"
- Treating your entire financial plan like a grad-level modeling assignment

You end up stuck in analysis. You stall because the plan isn't perfectly optimized. Meanwhile, time and opportunity slip away.

Why Engineers Oversimplify Money

On the flip side, engineers sometimes dismiss money as too basic:

- "Just spend less than you make."
- "Buy a house and you'll be fine."
- "Max out your 401(k). Done."

These statements are technically correct—but dangerously incomplete.

Oversimplification leads to:

- Neglecting risk (disability insurance, estate planning, etc.)
- Assuming one-size-fits-all strategies (e.g., always buying instead of renting)

- Underestimating tax impact (especially with RSUs or self-employment income)
- Forgetting to update your plan as life gets more complex

In the pursuit of efficiency, oversimplification can lead to **blind spots** that cost time, money, and peace of mind.

The Sweet Spot: Engineering-Inspired Simplicity

You don't need to over-engineer your finances. You also shouldn't treat them like a middle school math problem.

The sweet spot is: **systems-level thinking, simplified for real life.**

This means:

- Automating good behavior
- Focusing on big levers (saving rate, time horizon, diversification)
- Using checklists instead of 20-tab spreadsheets
- Revisiting your plan twice a year
- Asking for help when it's time to delegate

Think about your money like a versioned product release—not a one-time prototype.

Real-World Examples: Overcomplication in Action

Case 1: A 28-year-old engineer spends weeks comparing three index funds. The difference in returns over 30 years? Maybe $2,000. The cost of delay from not investing at all? $40,000.

Case 2: A 35-year-old engineer reads blogs arguing whether Roth or Traditional 401(k) is better. Analysis turns into paralysis. They miss out on 5 years of employer matching contributions.

Case 3: A 45-year-old engineer is obsessed with creating a custom asset allocation model. But they don't have an estate plan, disability coverage, or updated insurance. One accident would wreck their entire model.

Real-World Examples: Oversimplification in Action

Case 1: A 25-year-old engineer hears "buy real estate—it always appreciates." They purchase a house without considering maintenance costs, HOA fees, or how long they'll stay in the area. They end up underwater and frustrated.

Case 2: A 40-year-old engineer has been maxing out their 401(k) but never rebalances the portfolio. It's 90% tech stocks. When the market crashes, they lose 35% of their retirement savings in one year.

Case 3: A 55-year-old engineer assumes they're on track because they "make good money." But they've never projected how much they'll actually need in retirement. When they finally run the numbers, they're $600,000 behind.

Plain Language Breakdowns of Key Issues

ETFs and Expense Ratios: Yes, lower is better. But 0.03% vs. 0.06% won't make or break your future. Time in the market is more important than shaving decimal points.

401(k) vs Roth 401(k): Both are great. The key is to contribute early and often. You can split contributions between both. Don't let the debate keep you from saving.

Buying vs Renting: Buying a home is not always the best investment. Factor in time horizon, interest rates, job mobility, and maintenance before assuming it's always better.

Investing vs Paying Debt: If your debt interest rate is under 4%, and you have a long time horizon, investing often creates more long-term wealth. But emotions matter too—some engineers sleep better being debt-free.

Pros and Cons: Thinking Too Much vs Not Enough

Overcomplication Pros:

- Deep understanding of tools and systems
- High accuracy when a decision is made
- Often discover tax-saving or risk-management strategies

Overcomplication Cons:

- Delayed action = lost compounding
- Missed deadlines or contribution windows
- Burnout from constant tweaking

Oversimplification Pros:

- Fast action
- Less stress
- Easy to maintain routines

Oversimplification Cons:

- Blind to tax pitfalls, risk, or inefficiencies
- May ignore long-term shifts (inflation, changing family needs)
- Often leave money on the table

Action Steps to Find Your Financial Sweet Spot

1. **Audit your behavior**: Are you more prone to overthinking or oversimplifying?
2. **Pick 3 high-impact habits**: Examples: max out Roth IRA, automate savings, review insurance annually.
3. **Set decision deadlines**: Give yourself a time limit for research.

Example: "Choose an index fund in 72 hours."

4. **Use 80/20 thinking**: Focus on the 20% of decisions that create 80% of your results.
5. **Create a 1-page financial dashboard**: Net worth, monthly savings rate, investment allocation. Simpler = more usable.
6. **Ask for help**: Work with a financial advisor, CPA, or mentor when the decisions exceed your time or skill bandwidth.

A Moment of Encouragement

You don't need to be perfect with money. You just need to stay in the game long enough to benefit from your good habits.

You're already trained to think deeply. Now practice thinking *simply and clearly.*

You're more capable than you think.

The Takeaway

The smartest engineers know when to go deep—and when to keep it simple.

Your job is to **engineer your financial life to function well**, not to obsess over every detail or assume one-click decisions will work forever.

Model. Implement. Improve. Then step back and let the system run.

Final Note

This chapter isn't about pointing fingers—it's about building awareness.

You've likely overthought some things. You've probably glossed over others. That's normal. Now you know.

Money isn't about being the most clever. It's about:

- Staying consistent
- Avoiding big mistakes
- Building something that works—on your terms

Let's move forward with clarity, simplicity, and confidence.

Your system doesn't need to be perfect. It just needs to run.

Part II: Early Financial Foundations – Start Smart

The early stages of your career are when the financial blueprint of your life gets drawn—and small decisions now will ripple for decades.

Part II: Early Financial Foundations – Start Smart is designed to help engineers in their 20s and 30s lay down the building blocks of long-term financial stability. Whether you're just out of school or finally earning consistent income, this section will teach you how to take full control of your money with the same logic, precision, and planning you apply to engineering work.

These chapters break down how to read your first paycheck, set up a budget that actually fits your life, evaluate student loan strategies, understand the tradeoffs between paying down debt and investing, and begin building an emergency fund, credit history, and retirement accounts. We also explore the behavioral side of money—how to resist lifestyle inflation and peer pressure, how to set financial priorities, and how to automate your financial life so your system works even when you're busy.

By the end of this section, you'll know how to structure your cash flow, build a resilient system, and set financial habits that scale with your career and lifestyle. It's not about getting rich overnight—it's about starting right so you don't have to rebuild later.

If your career is a rocket, this is your launchpad.

And you only need to launch once—if you do it well.

Chapter 6: Understanding Your Paycheck and Employer Benefits

Let's start with something you receive regularly but may not fully understand: your paycheck.

You probably check the deposit amount, maybe glance at the taxes taken out, and move on. But embedded in your paycheck is the core of your financial life—income, deductions, taxes, and benefits that directly affect your future. As an engineer, your ability to decode and leverage this information can determine whether you're just getting paid… or truly building wealth.

This chapter is about helping you do more than cash your paycheck. It's about teaching you how to read it like a system diagram, optimize your withholdings, and maximize the benefits your employer is already offering you.

Why This Matters

Many engineers spend more time reviewing CAD drawings or debugging code than they ever spend looking at their pay stub or benefits portal. That's understandable—money isn't your main job.

But here's what you need to understand:

- Your **take-home pay** is only part of your compensation.
- Your **benefits** are worth thousands (sometimes tens of thousands) of

dollars per year.

- If you don't optimize what you're given, you're leaving money on the table.

And for engineers earning $70K, $120K, $200K or more, the stakes are too high to ignore.

Anatomy of a Paycheck

Let's start with the basics. Your paycheck typically includes:

- **Gross Pay** – Your total earnings before deductions.
- **Federal Income Tax** – Based on your tax bracket and withholding choices.
- **State Income Tax** – Depends on where you live (and sometimes where you work).
- **FICA Taxes** – Social Security and Medicare (usually 7.65%).
- **Other Deductions** – Health insurance premiums, 401(k) contributions, HSA/FSA contributions, life/disability insurance, stock purchases.

Now break it down:

Gross Pay vs Take-Home Pay: That $100K job offer doesn't mean $100K in your bank account. After taxes and benefits, your actual monthly take-home might be $5,800—or less.

Pre-Tax Contributions: Contributions to a traditional 401(k), HSA, or FSA reduce your taxable income. This lowers your federal and state tax bills.

Post-Tax Deductions: Some benefits, like Roth 401(k) or after-tax life insurance premiums, come out after taxes.

Federal and State Taxes: What's Actually Yours?

As an engineer, you should know how much of your income is truly "yours."

Your tax bracket doesn't mean everything is taxed at that rate. You're taxed **progressively**:

- The first portion of your income is taxed at 10%
- The next portion at 12%, then 22%, then 24%, and so on

Your Effective Tax Rate is the average rate you actually pay. **Your Marginal Tax Rate** is the rate at which your next dollar is taxed.

Understanding both helps you:

- Decide whether to use pre-tax or Roth contributions
- Plan for bonuses or raises
- Project what a side hustle or RSU vesting will do to your tax situation

Employer Benefits: Hidden Wealth Engines

Here's where things get interesting. Your **compensation package** includes more than salary. Let's break down the major areas you need to understand and optimize.

1. 401(k) or 403(b) Retirement Plans

These employer-sponsored retirement plans are often your **most powerful wealth-building tool**.

- **Contribution Limits:** $23,000/year (2025 limit), or $30,500 if 50+
- **Match:** Many companies match 3%–6% of your salary. This is free money.
- **Traditional vs Roth:** Traditional lowers taxes today. Roth grows tax-free for tomorrow.

Max out the match **at a minimum.**

2. Health Insurance

Health insurance is one of your biggest benefits. Plans include:

- **PPO:** More flexibility, higher premiums
- **HMO:** Lower cost, restricted providers
- **HDHP:** High deductible, but HSA-eligible

3. Health Savings Account (HSA)

If you're enrolled in an HDHP, this is one of the most powerful savings vehicles available:

- **Triple Tax Benefit**: Contributions are pre-tax, growth is tax-free, and withdrawals are tax-free for medical expenses
- **Portability:** Your HSA stays with you when you leave
- **Long-Term Growth:** Use it like a stealth IRA

4. Flexible Spending Accounts (FSA)

FSAs can help pay for health or childcare costs pre-tax—but use it or lose it. Know your deadlines.

5. Employee Stock Purchase Plan (ESPP)

Many engineers at public companies can buy company stock at a discount (often 10–15%). This can be a low-risk opportunity to earn extra returns—but only if you understand the rules around:

- Taxes
- Holding periods

- Sale strategy

6. Life and Disability Insurance

Your employer often provides basic life and disability insurance. Don't ignore this:

- **Disability Insurance** is income protection. If your brain or body can't do the job, this pays your bills.
- **Life Insurance** helps dependents if you pass away

Often, your employer policy isn't enough on its own—but it's a good base layer.

7. Other Perks

Engineers often overlook these, but they add up:

- Tuition reimbursement
- Commuter benefits
- Gym stipends
- Professional development budgets
- Relocation packages

Every dollar of value here increases your true compensation.

Real-World Engineering Scenarios

Scenario 1: You're a 24-year-old engineer earning $90K. You ignore your 401(k) because retirement feels far away. Your employer matches 5%. After 5 years, you've left $22,500 of free money on the table.

Scenario 2: You take the PPO plan "just to be safe." Your premiums are $3,000/year higher than the HDHP. You rarely use healthcare. You're wasting money and missing out on an HSA.

Scenario 3: Your company offers an ESPP with a 15% discount. You don't participate. The stock goes up 10% in six months. You missed a risk-free 25% return.

Scenario 4: You contribute to your 401(k) but never looked at the investment options. You're sitting in a money market fund earning 1% when you could be earning 7%+ long-term.

Action Steps

1. Pull your latest pay stub. Break it down: what are you paid, what are you taxed, what's being deducted?
2. Review your benefits portal. List every benefit your employer offers and what you're using.
3. Max out your 401(k) match if you're not already.
4. Consider switching to an HDHP + HSA if your health needs allow.
5. Revisit your tax withholding settings using IRS Form W-4.
6. Set up a 30-minute quarterly review of your paycheck and benefits usage.

Pros and Cons of Employer Benefit Optimization

Pros:

- Turns free benefits into wealth engines
- Lowers your tax burden
- Increases overall compensation
- Builds resilience against health or income shocks

Cons:

- Requires initial time and learning curve
- Choices can feel overwhelming at first

- Some benefits (like ESPP) carry risk if misused

Plain Language Concepts Demystified

Marginal Tax Brackets: Only the last dollars you earn are taxed at the highest rate. Your entire income isn't taxed at 32%.

HSA vs FSA: HSA rolls over and grows like an investment. FSA must be used by year-end (or grace period).

Employer Match: If your employer matches 5% and you're not contributing, you're giving yourself a pay cut.

Disability Insurance: Like a generator for your income stream. If your brain or back gives out, it keeps the lights on.

A Moment of Encouragement

You already have the skills to read a technical drawing or a system schematic. Your paycheck is just another data source. It tells the story of how your company values you—and how you can maximize that value.

Once you understand it, you can stop reacting and start planning.

You're more capable than you think.

The Takeaway

Engineers who understand their paycheck and benefits make better financial decisions, save more, and build wealth faster.

The smartest engineers don't just work for money—they know how to **leverage** every dollar they earn.

Final Note

This chapter wasn't about budgets or investments. It was about understanding what you already have access to.

This book isn't just about money. It's about:

- Owning your compensation
- Owning your future
- Building the life you want with tools already in your hands

Whether you're in your first year or your fifteenth, this chapter gives you control.

Use it.

Chapter 7: Budgeting Systems for Analytical Minds

Let's be honest—most budgeting advice out there isn't written for engineers.

It's vague. It's emotional. It talks about "manifesting" your goals or cutting lattes as a path to financial freedom. That's not helpful when your brain is wired for data, systems, and optimization.

So this chapter offers something different: a budgeting approach that treats your income like a resource allocation model. One that respects your time, adapts to your lifestyle, and helps you use your money with purpose.

Whether you're just starting out or trying to regain control in mid-career, budgeting is how you stop wondering where your money went—and start telling it exactly where to go.

What Budgeting Really Is

At its core, budgeting is not about restriction. It's not about guilt, shame, or spreadsheets filled with unrealistic expectations.

Budgeting is a **design tool**. It helps you:

- Direct limited resources toward your highest priorities
- Maintain system stability even under stress (job loss, unexpected expense)
- Optimize efficiency, control flow, and create long-term stability

Sound familiar? It should. Budgeting is **system engineering applied to cash flow**.

Why Engineers Often Struggle with Budgeting

You'd think engineers would be great at budgeting—but many aren't. Here's why:

1. **You expect precision**: If the budget doesn't work out *exactly*, you abandon it.
2. **You want optimization**: You spend too much time trying to create the "perfect" budget model.
3. **You get bored**: Budgeting feels like a repetitive admin task with no elegant solution.
4. **You're busy**: Between work, family, and side projects, money management gets deprioritized.
5. **You assume you're doing fine**: You make a good salary, so you think "it'll work itself out."

But without a plan, high income can still lead to poor outcomes.

The Engineer's Approach: Budgeting as Resource Allocation

Let's reframe budgeting as an engineering problem:

- **Inputs**: Salary, bonus, rental income, dividends
- **Fixed Outputs**: Rent/mortgage, insurance, loans, subscriptions
- **Variable Outputs**: Groceries, entertainment, dining, travel
- **Control Systems**: Automation, alerts, caps, tracking tools
- **Feedback Loops**: Monthly review, course correction, annual reset

Choosing the Right Budgeting Framework

There's no one-size-fits-all. But here are a few systems engineers tend to appreciate:

1. Zero-Based Budgeting

Every dollar is assigned a job—income minus expenses equals zero.
Best for:

- Engineers early in their careers
- Those who want granular control

Requires:

- High engagement
- Regular maintenance

2. The 50/30/20 Rule

- 50% to needs
- 30% to wants
- 20% to savings/debt

Best for:

- Engineers who want structure without micromanagement
- Those who need a simple launchpad

Requires:

- Some flexibility and awareness of category drift

3. Percentage-Based Bucketing

Set your own rules:

- 25% to fixed expenses
- 25% to investments
- 20% to discretionary
- 10% to long-term savings
- 10% to travel/fun
- 10% to future big goals (wedding, down payment, sabbatical)

Best for:

- Mid-career engineers with variable incomes or bonuses

Building Your Budget Step by Step

Step 1: Track Current Spending

Before you budget, you need data. Use Mint, YNAB, spreadsheets, or credit card statements. Categorize expenses for 30–90 days.

Look for:

- Recurring costs
- Surprise charges
- Areas that don't align with your values

Step 2: Calculate Net Monthly Income

Use **take-home pay**, not gross. Factor in bonuses only after they hit. If irregular, treat them as surplus to allocate manually.

Step 3: Identify Non-Negotiables

Rent/mortgage, loans, groceries, utilities, insurance. These are the immovable parts of your cash flow.

Step 4: Prioritize Goals

Where do you want your money to go *first*?

- Retirement?
- Emergency fund?
- Debt payoff?
- Investing for FIRE?

This is your mission directive.

Step 5: Build Your System

Now allocate each dollar based on your chosen framework. Keep it simple. Add complexity *after* you build consistency.

Automating Your Budget

Automation is your best friend.

- Direct deposit to multiple accounts
- Auto-transfer to savings/investments
- Credit card alerts and caps
- Auto-payments for recurring bills

Think of this as your **control system**—designed to reduce manual effort and emotional interference.

Budgeting for Variable Incomes

If you have bonuses, side gigs, or RSUs:

1. Base your core budget only on your salary
2. Treat extras as windfalls to allocate intentionally

Buckets might include:

- Tax reserve (for unwithheld income)
- Accelerated debt payments
- Roth IRA contributions
- Vacation fund
- Down payment or home maintenance

Real-World Engineering Scenarios

Scenario 1: A 26-year-old aerospace engineer wants to start investing but "can't find extra money." After tracking expenses, they realize $800/month is going to food delivery, bars, and online subscriptions. They reallocate half to a Roth IRA and automation does the rest.

Scenario 2: A 35-year-old software engineer with a $170K salary and $30K annual bonus uses a 70/30 split. Salary covers all basics + retirement. Bonus is split 50% toward brokerage investing, 30% toward a vacation, 20% into a home renovation fund.

Scenario 3: A 45-year-old systems engineer earning $220K with three kids needs clarity. They build a 1-page dashboard: income, fixed costs, savings rate, discretionary. Monthly review + quarterly goal tracking gives them peace of mind.

Pros and Cons of Budgeting Systems

Zero-Based Budgeting Pros:

- Maximum control
- Every dollar accounted for

Cons:

- Time intensive
- Easy to burn out

50/30/20 Pros:

- Simple
- Quick setup

Cons:

- Can feel too broad
- Less customization

Custom Buckets Pros:

- Tailored to your priorities
- Highly adaptable

Cons:

- Requires clarity up front
- May lead to drift without review

Tools Engineers Like

- Mint (free, automatic tracking)
- You Need A Budget (YNAB – rule-based, strong control logic)
- Tiller (spreadsheet-friendly)
- Excel or Google Sheets (fully customizable)
- Personal Capital (great for net worth + investments)

Pick one. Use it. Review monthly.

Action Steps

1. Choose a framework (zero-based, 50/30/20, or custom bucket)
2. Track your last 90 days of expenses
3. Set up a budget for the next 30 days
4. Automate one action this week (investment, bill, or savings)
5. Schedule a monthly 30-minute review session

Plain Language Breakdowns

Cash Flow: Money coming in vs going out—your personal current.

Discretionary Spending: Expenses you can adjust (e.g., travel, dining, clothes).

Fixed Costs: Bills that stay the same monthly (rent, loan payments).

Pay Yourself First: Save/invest automatically before spending anything.

Sinking Fund: Saving slowly for large, infrequent costs (e.g., car repairs, gifts, vacations).

A Moment of Encouragement

You don't need a perfect system. You need a system that **runs**.

Once your budget is dialed in, it becomes a launchpad—not a leash.

You're more capable than you think.

The Takeaway

The smartest engineers don't rely on luck or hope. They use models, systems, and data to make their lives work better.

Budgeting is no different.

Done right, it creates:

- Clarity
- Confidence
- Control

And those are the real engines of wealth.

Final Note

This chapter wasn't about cutting back. It was about building **intentionality** into your money.

This book isn't just about money. It's about:

- Taking ownership
- Building structure
- Creating freedom

Whether you're launching your career or recalibrating midstream, budgeting is how you align your finances with your values.

Let's build your budget like you build everything else: with logic, care, and the long game in mind.

Chapter 8: Managing Student Loans and Other Early Debt

Debt can feel like a weight strapped to your financial engine—especially early in your career when you're just gaining momentum. For engineers, student loans, auto loans, and even credit card debt can disrupt your systems, cloud your goals, and stall your progress before you get started.

But here's the thing: debt isn't just a financial burden—it's a solvable engineering challenge. With the right framework, you can assess it, model your options, choose a repayment strategy, and optimize your outcomes.

This chapter will walk you through how to think about debt with the same clarity and precision you'd bring to a design problem or systems issue at work. You'll learn how to evaluate interest rates, compare payoff strategies, balance investing vs debt reduction, and choose repayment methods that align with both logic and life.

Why Engineers Often Delay Debt Planning

Let's start with the common traps:

- You assume you'll "grow out of it" because your salary will increase.
- You avoid running the numbers because the balance is emotionally overwhelming.
- You read conflicting advice: "Pay it all down fast" vs "Invest and let the

debt ride."
- You overthink the optimization and never take action.

Sound familiar? Good. Let's simplify and systematize.

Step One: Inventory Your Debts

List every loan and line of credit you owe. Include:

- Student loans (federal and private)
- Credit cards
- Auto loans
- Personal loans
- Any deferred or employer-based tuition reimbursement agreements

For each, track:

- Balance
- Interest rate
- Minimum monthly payment
- Due date
- Term (when it ends)
- Whether it's fixed or variable

Now rank your debts by **interest rate**, not balance.

Why? Because interest rate is the cost of borrowing. That's your system's friction. We eliminate high-friction zones first.

Step Two: Understand Student Loan Types

Engineers often graduate with a mix of federal and private loans. Here's what you need to know:

Federal Loans

- **Subsidized**: No interest while in school or deferment
- **Unsubsidized**: Interest accrues immediately
- **PLUS Loans**: Higher interest, often used by parents
- **Consolidation Loans**: Combine federal loans into one

Federal loans offer flexible repayment plans:

- Standard 10-Year
- Graduated (increases over time)
- Income-Driven Repayment (IDR)
- Public Service Loan Forgiveness (PSLF) eligible

Private Loans

- No federal protections
- Interest rates vary by credit and cosigner
- Few forgiveness options
- May be worth refinancing if credit improves

Step Three: Evaluate Your Strategy — Aggressive Payoff vs Optimized Allocation

This is the engineer's dilemma:

- Should I pay off loans as fast as possible?
- Or should I invest while paying the minimum?

Let's model both.

Example: You owe $40,000 at 6.8%. Your expected long-term investment return is 7–8%.

- If you're disciplined, investing can yield more over time.
- But guaranteed debt payoff (especially above 6%) is a strong, risk-free return.

Here's a rule of thumb:

- If the loan is above 6%, lean toward aggressive payoff.
- If it's below 4%, consider minimum payments and invest the rest.
- Between 4–6%? Depends on your risk tolerance and career stability.

Step Four: Pick a Repayment System

Avalanche Method

- Pay minimum on all debts
- Put extra toward the **highest interest** loan
- Mathematically optimal

Snowball Method

- Pay minimum on all debts
- Put extra toward the **smallest balance** loan
- Builds momentum fast

Hybrid Engineering Approach

- Combine avalanche logic with psychological wins
- Prioritize high-interest loans first, but knock out one small win early

Step Five: Automate and Monitor

Don't budget manually every month. Engineers thrive on automation.

- Auto-pay minimums to avoid missed payments
- Auto-transfer debt snowball payments from your checking
- Review your loan dashboard quarterly
- Use apps like Undebt.it, Mint, or spreadsheet tools for visual tracking

Step Six: Consider Refinancing

If you have private loans or high-rate federal loans (and don't need forgiveness options), refinancing might help.

Look for:

- Lower interest rate
- Fixed over variable (if you value predictability)
- No fees or prepayment penalties

Only refinance federal loans if you're certain you don't need:

- IDR plans
- Forbearance or deferment
- PSLF eligibility

Other Early Career Debts: Car Loans, Credit Cards, Personal Loans

Car Loans

- Should not exceed 15% of your take-home pay
- Aim for low interest and short terms
- If rates are high (7%+), consider early payoff

Credit Cards

- Avoid carrying a balance
- If you have debt, this is usually your **#1 priority**
- Interest rates of 18–24% are massive drag

Personal Loans

- Often used for weddings, medical, emergencies
- Evaluate need before taking
- Consolidate if rates are favorable

Real-World Engineering Examples

Scenario 1: A 24-year-old with $45,000 in federal loans at 6.8% and a $70K job. They split extra income: 70% to debt, 30% to Roth IRA. Payoff in 4.5 years.

Scenario 2: A 30-year-old engineer with $80K in student debt at 5.2%. Credit score now 750. Refinances to 3.9% over 7 years. Saves $7,400 in interest.

Scenario 3: A 35-year-old with $12K credit card debt. Focuses on this before contributing to 401(k). Uses avalanche method + part-time side hustle. Debt-free in 11 months.

Pros and Cons

Aggressive Payoff Pros:

- Guaranteed return
- Psychological relief
- Lower long-term interest paid

Aggressive Payoff Cons:

- Less money invested early
- May delay retirement savings

Balanced Approach Pros:

- Flexibility
- Grows net worth faster
- Maintains liquidity

Balanced Approach Cons:

- Slower debt elimination
- Requires discipline

Action Steps

1. Inventory all debt with balances, rates, terms
2. Pick a primary strategy (avalanche, snowball, hybrid)
3. Choose 1–2 debts to eliminate in 12 months
4. Set up auto-pay and auto-transfer for snowball amount
5. Revisit strategy annually or after raises, bonuses

A Moment of Encouragement

You are not behind. You are not bad with money. You're simply working through a system.

Debt is not a character flaw. It's just a load you're going to redistribute, reduce, and remove—systematically.

You're more capable than you think.

Takeaway

The smartest engineers don't panic when a system is under pressure—they analyze it, optimize it, and improve it.

Debt is a temporary condition. What matters is how you manage it while building forward.

Final Note

This chapter wasn't about shame. It was about strategy.

You don't need to be debt-free tomorrow. You just need to take control today.

This book isn't just about money. It's about:

- Making peace with your financial past
- Taking full ownership of your future
- Designing a system that frees you—not traps you

Let's move forward, one payment, one decision, one engineered outcome at a time.

Chapter 9: Emergency Funds – Designing Your Safety Net

Imagine you're running a high-performance machine. It's optimized for speed, efficiency, and output. Now imagine that same machine without any fail-safes, no buffer zones, and no backup system. One voltage spike, one overheating coil, and the whole thing shuts down.

That's your financial life without an emergency fund.

An emergency fund isn't exciting. It won't grow your wealth like an index fund or pay dividends like a rental property. But it's the unsung hero of financial systems—the thing that keeps your plan running when life gets bumpy.

As an engineer, you already understand the value of redundancy, buffers, and safety margins. So in this chapter, we'll build your emergency fund like you'd build a backup power system: stable, reliable, and ready when needed.

Why Emergency Funds Matter

Before we talk about how much or where to put it, let's talk about why it matters.

Because no matter how smart you are, how stable your job seems, or how many contingencies you've planned for—life will throw surprises at you. And they won't care about your timeline.

An emergency fund buys you:

- Time to find a new job if laid off
- Space to make good decisions under pressure
- Protection against derailing your investment plan
- Control in moments where others panic

Without one, a $2,000 car repair becomes credit card debt. A layoff turns into a 401(k) withdrawal. A medical bill forces a loan against your HSA.

It's not just about money. It's about keeping your system intact.

What Qualifies as an Emergency?

Let's define terms.

An emergency is:

- **Unexpected**: You didn't plan for it
- **Unavoidable**: You can't push it off
- **Unbudgeted**: It's not part of your monthly plan

Examples:

- Job loss
- Medical expense
- Major car or home repair
- Family emergency travel
- Legal or tax issue

Not emergencies:

- Concert tickets
- Holiday gifts
- Annual subscription renewals
- Car maintenance you knew was coming

Your emergency fund is not your convenience fund.

How Much Do You Need?

This depends on your risk profile, career field, and personal obligations. But here's a general guide:

Minimum Buffer: 1 month of expenses **Standard Safety Net:** 3–6 months of essential expenses **High Resilience Fund:** 6–12 months for:

- Freelancers
- One-income households
- High-risk industries

Start with one month. Build to three. Then aim for six.

Remember: this isn't six months of your income. It's six months of **necessary spending.** That includes:

- Rent/mortgage
- Utilities
- Insurance
- Food
- Debt minimums
- Transportation

Not included:

- Travel
- Entertainment
- Dining out
- Roth IRA contributions

Where to Keep It

You want accessibility and safety—not growth.

Best options:

- High-yield savings account
- Online money market account
- Credit union account

Avoid:

- Stock market (too volatile)
- CDs with long lock-in periods
- Retirement accounts (penalties + paperwork)

Your emergency fund isn't an investment. It's insurance.

How to Build It Step-by-Step

Step 1: Calculate Monthly Essentials

List your true monthly burn rate. This is your emergency baseline. Let's say it's $3,000.

Step 2: Set Milestones

- Month 1: $1,000 starter buffer
- Month 2–6: Build to 3 months ($9,000)
- Bonus months: Add 1 month each quarter until 6–12

Step 3: Automate the Build

Set up a dedicated savings account. Auto-transfer a fixed amount each payday—start with $50 or $100. Scale up with raises.

Step 4: Use Windfalls

Tax return? Bonus? Birthday money? Send 10–50% to your fund until it's fully built.

Step 5: Replenish Immediately After Use

This isn't a one-time project. If you use the fund, rebuilding becomes top priority.

Real-World Engineering Examples

Scenario 1: A 25-year-old software engineer lives in a tech hub. Rent is high. Job stability is solid but not guaranteed. They build 4 months of expenses ($12K) over 18 months using auto-savings and 20% of each bonus.

Scenario 2: A 35-year-old civil engineer has a spouse and two kids. They carry a mortgage and one car loan. They target 6 months of core expenses ($24K). Keep $18K in high-yield savings and $6K in a separate checking buffer.

Scenario 3: A 45-year-old systems engineer makes $200K. They run lean, but worry about a corporate restructure. They keep $50K in emergency reserves split across two institutions.

Scenario 4: A 60-year-old mechanical engineer prepping for retirement holds $40K in cash equivalents to avoid withdrawing from investments during a market downturn.

Pros and Cons of Emergency Funds

Pros:

- Peace of mind
- Prevents credit card debt
- Buys time during disruption
- Keeps investment plans intact

Cons:

- Low return compared to market
- Tempting to misuse without discipline
- Requires patience to build

Action Steps

1. List your monthly core expenses
2. Set your emergency fund target (3–6 months)
3. Open a high-yield savings account
4. Automate weekly or monthly contributions
5. Track progress on your net worth sheet
6. Replenish immediately after any usage

Plain Language Concepts

Emergency Fund: Your financial safety net. Not for investing. Not for shopping. For real, unexpected problems only.

High-Yield Savings Account: An online savings account offering more interest than traditional banks (often 4%+).

Cash Buffer: Extra money in checking or savings to avoid overdraft or credit use.

Liquidity: How fast you can access your money. Emergency funds must be highly liquid.

A Moment of Encouragement

You may not feel wealthy yet—but having a fully funded emergency fund puts you ahead of the majority of Americans.

It's not flashy. But it's foundational.

You're more capable than you think.

The Takeaway

The smartest engineers don't build systems without buffers.

And they don't build wealth without a safety net.

An emergency fund won't make you rich—but it protects everything that will.

Final Note

This chapter wasn't about fear. It was about **resilience**.

This book isn't just about money. It's about:

- Keeping your life on track when things go sideways
- Giving yourself options in times of stress
- Building peace of mind as well as wealth

Whether you're just starting out or heading into retirement, your emergency fund is the firewall protecting your future.

Build it like your financial life depends on it—because someday, it might.

Part III: Saving and Investing – Setting Your Systems to Work

This is where your money stops sitting still and starts pulling its weight.

Part III: Saving and Investing – Setting Your Systems to Work is all about turning your income into a tool for long-term freedom. Whether you're just starting to save or ready to invest beyond your 401(k), this section gives engineers a structured, data-informed roadmap to build lasting wealth—without getting lost in financial jargon or hype.

These chapters walk you through everything from basic account types and investment vehicles to risk management, asset allocation, and long-term portfolio design. You'll learn how to automate your savings, how to choose between traditional and Roth accounts, how to handle stock options and equity compensation, and how to optimize for tax efficiency without overcomplicating your life. We also cover real-world decision points—like whether to pay off debt or invest, how to handle market volatility, and how to adjust your strategy as life evolves.

By the end of Part III, you'll have a financial engine that runs steadily in the background—built for resilience, simplicity, and growth. Your job isn't to predict the market. It's to build a system that works whether the market is up, down, or sideways.

You've done the hard part—earning the income. Now it's time to put that money to work.

Chapter 10: The Real Cost of Lifestyle Inflation

Let's start with a question: If you double your salary, should you double your lifestyle?

For many engineers, the answer feels obvious—yes. More income means more options. A better car, a bigger house, upgraded gadgets, better vacations. It feels like the natural reward for years of hard work.

But here's the truth: **Lifestyle inflation is one of the quietest, most dangerous threats to your financial future.**

It creeps in slowly. It feels good. It's socially reinforced. But over time, it erodes your savings rate, shrinks your future options, and locks you into higher expenses that are hard to reverse.

This chapter is not about guilt. It's about awareness. It's about putting structure around your spending choices so that your growing income leads to **freedom**, not just fancier problems.

What Is Lifestyle Inflation?

Lifestyle inflation happens when your spending increases at the same rate—or faster—than your income.

Your expenses rise as you:

- Move to a nicer apartment
- Lease a newer car

- Buy more expensive groceries
- Dine out more often
- Upgrade your tech, clothes, or gym
- Take on a higher mortgage or private school tuition

And each upgrade feels justified.

You're not splurging—you're "leveling up."

But each time you inflate your base lifestyle, you also increase:

- The monthly income you *need* to cover bills
- The size of your emergency fund
- The timeline to financial independence
- The psychological pressure to keep earning at a high level

Why Engineers Are Especially Vulnerable

Engineers tend to:

- Start with student debt
- Get significant income jumps early in their career
- Live in high-cost urban areas
- Work in cultures where success is visibly rewarded (e.g., cars, watches, homes)
- View spending as "earned" after intense problem-solving or long hours

You're smart. You solve complex problems all day. And you may feel like you "deserve" to enjoy your money.

You do.

But lifestyle inflation isn't enjoying your money. It's unintentionally spending more without improving long-term satisfaction or freedom.

Real Costs of Lifestyle Inflation

1. Longer Time to Financial Independence

If you spend $60K/year, you need $1.5M to retire (assuming the 4% rule). If you spend $100K/year, you need $2.5M.

That's a million-dollar lifestyle difference.

2. Reduced Flexibility

Bigger mortgage = less ability to take time off, pivot jobs, or weather downturns.

3. Increased Stress

You're making more—but spending more—so you *still* feel broke.

4. Missed Wealth-Building Opportunities

Every extra $1,000 you spend now could be $10,000+ in 20 years.

Lifestyle Inflation vs. Lifestyle Design

Inflation is unconscious. It happens without planning. Design is intentional. You choose what to spend on based on your values.

Engineers should design their lifestyles like they design systems:

- With constraints
- With purpose
- With long-term performance in mind

You don't need to live like a monk. But you do need to understand trade-offs.

Real-World Scenarios

Scenario 1: A 28-year-old engineer gets a $20K raise. They move into a luxury apartment and upgrade their car lease. Savings rate? Unchanged.

Scenario 2: A 35-year-old with kids upgrades from a $400K to $700K home. School is better, but their emergency fund target doubles and they're forced to cut back retirement savings.

Scenario 3: A 40-year-old software engineer earning $250K is maxed out every month. Despite a high income, they feel like they're barely treading water due to inflated lifestyle costs.

How to Fight Lifestyle Inflation

1. Set a Target Savings Rate

Engineers should aim for 20–30% of gross income saved.

Every raise? Increase savings first.

2. Delay Gratification by 3–6 Months

Before upgrading anything (car, house, watch), wait. If you still want it after the waiting period, proceed—intentionally.

3. Automate Savings Increases

Every raise triggers a bump in 401(k), brokerage, or HSA contributions.

4. Run "What If" Models

If you spend $3,000/month vs $5,000/month—what does that do to your retirement timeline?

Model it. Then decide.

5. Build Guilt-Free Spending Buckets

Set aside 5–10% of income for fun, upgrades, and luxuries. This keeps your lifestyle flexible without derailing your plan.

6. Track Your Savings Rate Annually

It's not your income that determines wealth—it's your savings rate.

Pros and Cons of Resisting Lifestyle Inflation

Pros:

- Faster wealth-building
- More job flexibility
- Less financial stress
- Stronger net worth over time

Cons:

- Feels like you're "behind" peers
- May need to say no to some upgrades
- Requires intentional tracking

Plain Language Concepts

Savings Rate: Percentage of your gross income saved or invested annually.

Lifestyle Creep: The slow, often unnoticed increase in your spending over time.

FIRE Number: How much you need to retire early based on your annual spending.

Golden Handcuffs: High-paying job you can't leave due to lifestyle dependencies.

Action Steps

1. Calculate your current savings rate
2. Compare current lifestyle cost vs 5 years ago
3. Pick one lifestyle upgrade to delay or downgrade
4. Model your FIRE number at different spending levels
5. Build a 3-tier spending plan: essential, flexible, luxury

A Moment of Encouragement

You don't need to deny yourself everything. You just need to align your spending with your vision—not with pressure, habit, or comparison.

You're more capable than you think.

The Takeaway

The smartest engineers understand that every system has a trade-off.

Spending more today often means giving up freedom tomorrow.

Live well. But live intentionally.

Final Note

This chapter wasn't about saying no to joy. It was about saying yes to freedom.

This book isn't just about money. It's about:

- Making thoughtful upgrades
- Avoiding autopilot spending
- Designing a lifestyle that serves you—not the other way around

Whether you're making $60K or $260K, the real question isn't "What can I afford?"

It's: "What am I building with this income?"

Make sure the answer is something that lasts.

Chapter 11: The Power of Compounding – Your Best Engineering Ally

Ask most engineers what their most powerful tool is, and you'll hear answers like mathematics, modeling, systems design, or logic.

But in personal finance, your most powerful tool is time.

And when paired with a system that grows on itself over time—like compounding—it becomes a force multiplier. One that can outpace salaries, bonuses, promotions, and even your smartest budgeting strategies.

This chapter is about understanding compound growth the same way you'd understand exponential stress in a system. What begins as slow, almost imperceptible movement becomes unstoppable over time—if left uninterrupted.

Let's build a system that compounds your financial progress the way great engineers compound their designs—efficiently, elegantly, and with long-term momentum.

What Is Compounding?

Compounding is the process where your earnings (from investments or interest) generate their own earnings. It's **growth on top of growth**. You earn money not just on your original principal, but also on the interest or returns you've already received.

In engineering terms: compounding is positive feedback in a closed system—when the output loops back in and fuels the next iteration.

It's what transforms small, consistent actions into massive long-term outcomes.

Why Compounding Matters More Than Income

High income helps. But income without investment doesn't create wealth. It just creates lifestyle.

Compound growth, by contrast, creates freedom.

Here's why:

- Time > Rate of Return > Contributions
- Starting earlier beats starting with more
- Interruptions (like withdrawals or waiting to invest) are more damaging than people realize

Example:

- Start investing $500/month at age 25. Stop at age 35. Total invested: $60,000.
- Let it sit until 65. Final balance: ~$500,000 (assuming 8% return)

Now take someone who starts at 35 and invests $500/month until 65.

- Total invested: $180,000
- Final balance: ~$600,000

Both end up in similar places, but the early starter invested a **third as much**.

Time is the multiplier.

Where Compounding Happens

You'll see the power of compounding in:

- Stock market returns
- Bond interest
- Real estate appreciation with reinvested cash flow
- Retirement accounts (401(k), Roth IRA, HSA)
- Business equity that reinvests profits

But compounding can also work **against** you:

- Credit card debt
- Student loan interest (especially unsubsidized)
- Any interest-bearing loan where balance grows over time

The key is to make compounding your employee—not your enemy.

How Engineers Undervalue Compounding

Here's the trap:

- Engineers focus on precision and optimization
- They delay action in favor of more research
- They wait for the "right time" to start investing

But compounding rewards **action over perfection**.

The most important decision is not what to invest in—it's **when to begin**.

Start imperfectly. Adjust along the way. Let time do the heavy lifting.

Building a Compounding System

Step 1: Automate Consistent Contributions

- Pick a percentage of your income (10–20%)
- Set it to flow into retirement accounts, brokerage, or HSA automatically

Step 2: Choose Investments That Grow

- Focus on broad-market index funds or ETFs
- Avoid high fees, unnecessary complexity, or speculative picks

Step 3: Leave It Alone

- The more you tinker, the more you interrupt the compounding process
- Resist the urge to time the market

Step 4: Reinvest Earnings

- If your account pays dividends or interest, reinvest automatically

Step 5: Increase Contributions With Income

- Every time you get a raise, bump up your contributions by 1–2%

Step 6: Track Net Worth, Not Daily Returns

- Focus on long-term growth
- Ignore day-to-day market noise

Real-World Scenarios for Engineers

Scenario 1: A 27-year-old software engineer invests $300/month in a Roth IRA. After 20 years, their balance is $180K. After 35 years, it's $650K. They didn't change jobs. They just stayed consistent.

Scenario 2: A 42-year-old mechanical engineer gets a $25,000 bonus. Instead of spending it all, they invest half in a diversified fund. That $12,500 grows to over $67,000 by retirement.

Scenario 3: A 60-year-old nearing retirement starts late and panics. They invest aggressively, but volatility leads to emotional mistakes. The lesson? Compounding favors **early and steady**—not late and frantic.

Plain Language Breakdown of Key Concepts

Compound Interest: Money you earn on your previous interest or returns.

Annualized Return: The average rate of return per year over a period of time.

Reinvestment: Putting your dividends, interest, or capital gains back into your portfolio.

Dollar-Cost Averaging: Investing a fixed amount consistently, regardless of market price.

Time Horizon: The length of time you plan to invest before using the money.

Pros and Cons of Compounding as a Wealth Strategy

Pros:

- Doesn't require high income
- Doesn't depend on perfect timing
- Benefits grow exponentially over time
- Supports early retirement and financial independence

Cons:

- Requires patience
- Takes time to "feel" like it's working
- Is sensitive to disruptions (withdrawals, fear-based selling)

Action Steps

1. Open a retirement or investment account (if you haven't already)
2. Set up automatic contributions—even $100/month is powerful
3. Choose a low-cost index fund to start
4. Check your portfolio quarterly, not daily
5. Commit to reinvesting all earnings
6. Use a compound growth calculator to model future value

A Moment of Encouragement

Compounding is boring at first. Then it becomes unbelievable.

You're not going to "feel" wealthy in year two or three. But stick with it, and year fifteen will make your jaw drop.

You're more capable than you think. And your money is more powerful than you realize—if you give it time.

The Takeaway

Engineers love leverage. Compounding is financial leverage.

It turns time into growth, and small decisions into massive outcomes.

If you want to build wealth as an engineer, forget about picking the next big stock or perfectly timing the market.

Build a system that compounds. Feed it. Leave it alone. Let it grow.

Final Note

This chapter wasn't about theory. It was about force.

Compounding is a force multiplier in your life—just like in systems design.

This book isn't just about money. It's about:

- Taking small actions now for massive payoffs later
- Leveraging time as your greatest ally
- Trusting the system you build

Whether you're in year one or year twenty of your career, the best time to start compounding is now.

Start where you are. And keep going.

Chapter 12: How to Think About Risk Like an Engineer

Let's start by stating the obvious: you already think about risk every day.

You do it when designing a bridge, writing code for a mission-critical system, or building a product that millions of people will use. In engineering, risk isn't emotional. It's something to measure, model, mitigate, and monitor.

Now let's take that same mindset—and apply it to money.

Risk is everywhere in personal finance. Not just in the stock market, but in your income stream, your insurance decisions, your investment allocations, and your retirement planning timeline. Most people either ignore risk entirely or fear it so much that they avoid action altogether.

But you're not most people. You're an engineer.

You've trained yourself to work through uncertainty with structure. This chapter will help you transfer that skill into your financial life.

What Is Risk, Really?

Risk is not just "losing money."

In engineering and in finance, risk is the **possibility of a deviation from expected outcomes**—especially negative ones.

That could mean:

- Losing your job unexpectedly
- Getting sick or injured
- Outliving your savings
- Missing your investment target
- Being underinsured in a critical situation
- Buying into hype and making a poor investment

Risk is part of the game. Your job is not to eliminate it. Your job is to understand it, reduce what can be reduced, and be prepared for what remains.

Risk in Engineering vs. Risk in Finance

In engineering, you might use:

- FMEA (Failure Modes and Effects Analysis)
- Redundancy
- Load testing
- Stress modeling

In finance, we use:

- Diversification
- Emergency funds
- Insurance
- Asset allocation
- Time horizon matching

The principles overlap:

1. Don't rely on a single point of failure
2. Accept that failure isn't always preventable—but damage can be minimized

3. Design systems to withstand worst-case inputs
4. Simulate outcomes before they happen

So if you've used Monte Carlo simulations or stress testing in your work—you're more prepared for financial planning than you think.

Types of Financial Risk

Here are the key categories engineers should recognize:

1. Market Risk

The value of your investments may decline due to market fluctuations.

2. Inflation Risk

Your money may lose purchasing power over time.

3. Longevity Risk

You might live longer than your money lasts.

4. Liquidity Risk

You might need to access funds when they're not available.

5. Income Risk

Your job or business income might change unexpectedly.

6. Concentration Risk

Too much of your wealth might be tied up in one asset (e.g., company stock).

7. Behavioral Risk

You might react emotionally and make poor decisions (e.g., panic selling).

Building a Risk-Resilient Financial System

Just like engineering systems need fault tolerance, so does your financial life. Here's how:

1. Diversify Everything

- Don't own just one type of investment
- Don't rely on just one income stream
- Don't keep all your cash in one bank

2. Insure Intelligently

- Disability insurance = backup generator for your income
- Life insurance = financial protection for those who depend on you
- Umbrella insurance = wide-range protection from liability lawsuits

3. Maintain Liquidity Buffers

- Emergency fund = cash reservoir for system shocks
- Keep 3–6 months of core expenses liquid and accessible

4. Use Time as an Ally

- Long investment horizons reduce short-term market risk
- Match short-term goals with low-risk instruments (e.g., savings, short bonds)

5. Avoid Over-Engineering

Don't paralyze yourself by chasing a "perfect" plan.

Sometimes 80% correct and executed is better than 100% accurate but never implemented.

How Engineers Tend to Misunderstand Risk

1. Overconfidence in Predictive Models

Finance is more probabilistic than deterministic. Markets, inflation, job security—all have uncertainty you can't fully control.

2. Underinsurance

Engineers tend to self-insure because they trust their income—but fail to plan for disruption.

3. Overconcentration in Company Stock

Equity compensation can be a gift or a trap. You're already employed by your company. Don't double down with all your net worth there.

4. Avoidance of Volatility

Volatility isn't the same as loss. Markets fluctuate, and downturns are normal. If you have a long time horizon, volatility is the **price of admission** for long-term returns.

Risk Tools You Can Actually Use

Monte Carlo Simulations

- Used in engineering. Also used in financial planning.
- Shows probabilities of success based on thousands of possible outcomes.
- Useful for retirement planning and goal setting.

Scenario Planning

- Build best-case, base-case, and worst-case budgets.
- Run through what happens if you lose your job, take a pay cut, or need to fund a family emergency.

FIRE Number Calculation

- Determine how much you need to retire safely.
- Based on expected spending, adjusted for inflation, and withdrawal rate (usually 4%).

Real-World Examples

Scenario 1: A 29-year-old electrical engineer puts 80% of net worth in employer RSUs. Stock drops 60% during a bear market. Their net worth is cut in half.

Scenario 2: A 40-year-old civil engineer has no disability insurance.

A skiing accident keeps them out of work for a year. Emergency fund is depleted in 5 months.

Scenario 3: A 60-year-old engineer is 100% in equities. They retire and the market drops 25% in the first year. They're forced to sell assets at a loss.

Action Steps to Manage Financial Risk

1. Run a Monte Carlo simulation for your retirement plan
2. Check your current investment allocation. Is it diversified?
3. Purchase or review disability insurance coverage
4. List all sources of income. How many are vulnerable?
5. Rebalance your 401(k) and brokerage accounts annually
6. Review concentration in any single asset (like employer stock)
7. Write out your worst-case scenario. What would you do?
8. Build a 12-month backup plan

Pros and Cons of Taking Financial Risks

Pros:

- Potential for higher returns
- Growth of wealth over time
- Achieving financial independence faster

Cons:

- Short-term volatility
- Psychological stress
- Possibility of losses if not properly managed

Plain Language Concepts Explained

Risk Tolerance – How much market fluctuation you can emotionally and financially handle.

Risk Capacity – How much risk you can afford to take based on your financial situation.

Volatility – Short-term up-and-down movement in asset values.

Diversification – Not putting all your eggs in one basket.

Asset Allocation – Choosing how much to invest in stocks, bonds, cash, real estate, etc.

A Moment of Encouragement

You already understand risk better than most people.

You model it, measure it, and mitigate it in your work. Your job now is to carry that expertise over into your personal finances.

You're more capable than you think.

The Takeaway

Risk isn't the enemy. Unmeasured, unmanaged risk is.

The smartest engineers don't avoid uncertainty. They design systems that can thrive in it.

So build your financial life like a resilient bridge. Account for wind. Expect stress. Add redundancy. Then move forward confidently.

Final Note

This chapter wasn't about fear. It was about control.

This book isn't just about money. It's about:

- Planning for what you can't predict
- Reducing what you can't afford to lose

- Accepting volatility without losing your footing

Whether you're earning your first paycheck or preparing to leave the workforce, your ability to think clearly about risk will shape every financial decision you make.

Model it. Manage it. Keep building.

Chapter 13: Building Your First Investment Portfolio

If you've made it this far in the book, then you already understand that financial systems matter. You get that time, discipline, and compounding are more powerful than stock-picking tips or financial clickbait.

Now it's time to apply what you know. This chapter is about creating something functional, something reliable, something that grows with you—your first investment portfolio.

But don't let the word "portfolio" intimidate you. A portfolio isn't a collection of secret formulas or flashy trends. It's a reflection of your goals, your values, your timeline, and your tolerance for uncertainty. It's a system—and you, as an engineer, are uniquely suited to design it.

So let's get to work.

Start With Your Goal, Not the Market

Too many investors jump into portfolio design backward. They ask, "What should I invest in?" before asking, "What am I trying to achieve?"

Your portfolio is a tool. It should serve a purpose. So begin by defining what you're investing for:

- Retirement (early or traditional)?
- Buying a home in 5–10 years?

- Building long-term generational wealth?
- Achieving financial independence (FIRE)?

Be specific. Know the time horizon and dollar amount needed. This determines everything that follows.

Understand Your Risk Tolerance and Risk Capacity

You can't engineer a stable structure without understanding its load limits. In finance, that means risk.

- **Risk tolerance** is emotional: How much loss can you stomach before panicking?
- **Risk capacity** is mathematical: How much loss can your finances withstand without blowing up your plan?

Know both. You don't want a portfolio that performs well on paper but keeps you up at night.

Asset Classes: The Building Blocks

Just like in engineering, systems perform best when they use the right components for the right job. Here are the primary materials:

1. Stocks (Equities)

- High return potential, higher volatility
- Best for long-term growth (10+ years)
- Can be domestic, international, large-cap, small-cap

2. Bonds (Fixed Income)

- Lower return, but more stable
- Provide income and reduce portfolio volatility
- Useful for shorter timeframes or conservative goals

3. Cash & Equivalents

- Liquid, safe, but earns little to no return
- Necessary for short-term expenses and emergency funds

4. Real Assets (Real Estate, REITs, etc.)

- Tangible, inflation-protected, often income-producing
- Can diversify your portfolio beyond stocks and bonds

5. Alternatives (Commodities, Crypto, Private Equity)

- High risk, high variance
- Use sparingly unless you're highly experienced

Asset Allocation: Your Portfolio's Blueprint

Now you're deciding how much of each building material to use. This is your **asset allocation**—and it determines more than 90% of your portfolio's performance.

General Guidelines:

- **Aggressive (under 35)**: 90% stocks / 10% bonds
- **Balanced (35–50)**: 70% stocks / 30% bonds
- **Conservative (50+)**: 50% stocks / 50% bonds (or less)

Note: These are starting points. You'll adjust based on your personal plan, not your age alone.

Use the **Rule of 100** or **Rule of 110**: Subtract your age from 100 or 110. That's the % of your portfolio that can be in stocks.

Account Selection: Tax Optimization

You wouldn't use a high-friction material where you need low resistance. Same principle applies here.

Different accounts serve different tax and liquidity purposes:

- **401(k)/403(b)** – Pre-tax, great for long-term savings
- **Roth IRA** – Post-tax, tax-free growth, ideal for early career savers
- **Traditional IRA** – Pre-tax (if deductible), grows tax-deferred
- **HSA** – Triple tax advantage, use for health costs or future spending
- **Taxable Brokerage Account** – Flexible, but taxed on gains

Use tax-advantaged accounts first. Fill your Roth and 401(k) buckets before turning to taxable accounts.

Simplicity Over Complexity: The Three-Fund Portfolio

You don't need 10 mutual funds or 25 individual stocks. In fact, most investors would do better with just three:

1. **Total U.S. Stock Market Index Fund** (VTI, FSKAX)
2. **Total International Stock Market Index Fund** (VXUS, FTIHX)
3. **Total Bond Market Fund** (BND, FXNAX)

This gives you global diversification, low fees, and simplicity.

Rebalance once a year.

Real-World Scenarios for Engineers

Case Study 1 – Entry-Level Software Engineer, Age 24:

- Roth IRA: $6,500/year in 90% stock / 10% bond index funds
- 401(k): 8% to get full employer match
- Cash buffer for 3–6 months expenses

Case Study 2 – Mid-Career Civil Engineer, Age 38:

- Max 401(k) contributions ($23,000)
- Roth IRA: Funded after 401(k)
- Taxable account for flexibility and early retirement goals

Case Study 3 – Systems Engineer, Age 50, Late Start:

- Catch-up contributions to 401(k) and IRA
- Conservative 60/40 portfolio
- Uses HSA to bridge healthcare gap in early retirement

Common Mistakes to Avoid

- Overweighting employer stock
- Reacting emotionally to market drops
- Ignoring fees and expense ratios
- Chasing performance instead of sticking to your plan
- Neglecting to rebalance

Action Steps

1. Clarify your financial goal and timeline
2. Assess your risk tolerance honestly
3. Choose a target asset allocation

4. Open the right accounts (start with Roth IRA or 401(k))
5. Pick low-cost index funds to match your allocation
6. Automate monthly contributions
7. Rebalance annually
8. Track net worth quarterly—not daily returns

A Moment of Encouragement

You don't need to be perfect to build wealth. You need to start. You need to keep going. You need to trust the structure you're building.

The smartest engineers don't reinvent the wheel every year. They design something solid and let time prove it right.

The Takeaway

Building your first investment portfolio is not about being flashy. It's not about finding a unicorn stock or calling the next crash.

It's about building a durable system.

It's about:

- Understanding the variables
- Choosing a strategy you can live with
- Minimizing friction (fees, taxes, emotion)
- Letting compounding do its job

Your portfolio should grow with you, not outpace your understanding.

Design it with care. Revisit it with discipline. And let it do the heavy lifting.

Final Note

This chapter wasn't just about investing. It was about designing a system that serves you.

This book isn't just about money. It's about:

- Building a life of options
- Creating stability through structure
- Thinking long-term without losing sight of now

Whether you're managing $1,000 or $1 million, your first portfolio isn't about the money. It's about the mindset and method that will compound for decades to come.

So start building. And don't stop.

Chapter 14: Stocks, Bonds, Real Estate, and Alternative Investments

Every system has its components.

For engineers, this is second nature. Before you simulate performance, optimize a load path, or test redundancy, you inventory your materials. The same is true in financial systems. Before you build a portfolio or make decisions that shape your financial future, you need to understand the raw materials of investing—your asset classes.

This chapter is your engineering guide to the four major asset classes: stocks, bonds, real estate, and alternative investments.

You'll learn how each works, what role it plays, and how to evaluate trade-offs. You don't need to become an expert in every asset class. You just need to know what each one can (and can't) do for you—and how to align those attributes with your personal goals, timelines, and risk tolerance.

STOCKS: THE ENGINE OF LONG-TERM GROWTH

Stocks are the equity component of your portfolio. They offer partial ownership in companies and represent your share in the future earnings of a business. Stocks are powerful, volatile, and—historically—the highest performing asset over time.

What You Own:

- A fractional share of a public company
- A claim to profits (dividends) and company growth (price appreciation)

Why They Matter:

- They offer the highest expected returns of all major assets
- They are critical for beating inflation over multi-decade periods
- They expose your money to business productivity, innovation, and global growth

How to Invest:

- Individual stocks (risky unless you're well-researched)
- Index funds (e.g., S&P 500, Total Market)
- ETFs (Exchange-Traded Funds)

Engineering Analogy:

Stocks are the dynamic loads in your portfolio. They fluctuate. They move. They require bracing (diversification) and periodic recalibration (rebalancing).

BONDS: THE STRUCTURAL SUPPORT

Bonds provide income and stability. They are loans you make to governments, municipalities, or corporations, who in turn pay you interest for a set period.

What You Own:

- A fixed-income contract with a maturity date
- Predictable income from coupon payments

Why They Matter:

- Provide ballast in volatile markets
- Stabilize portfolio drawdowns
- Can fund short-term goals with lower risk

How to Invest:

- U.S. Treasuries (safe, low return)
- Corporate bonds (riskier, higher return)
- Bond funds (e.g., Total Bond Market Fund)

Engineering Analogy:

Bonds are like structural steel—they add mass and stability. They may not excite, but when the wind picks up (markets crash), they keep the frame from buckling.

REAL ESTATE: THE TANGIBLE PERFORMER

Real estate includes property—residential, commercial, or industrial—that generates income, appreciates, or both. You can own it directly or through financial instruments like REITs.

What You Own:

- Direct: the property itself
- Indirect: shares in a company or fund that owns/manage properties

Why It Matters:

- Generates rental income
- Typically appreciates with inflation
- Offers tax advantages (depreciation, 1031 exchanges)
- Provides portfolio diversification

How to Invest:

- Buy and rent physical property
- Public REITs (Real Estate Investment Trusts)
- Private real estate platforms (Fundrise, RealtyMogul)

Engineering Analogy:

Real estate is a high-mass component. It's load-bearing but inflexible. It performs well under pressure but lacks liquidity.

ALTERNATIVE INVESTMENTS: THE EXPERIMENTAL MODULE

These include any asset that doesn't fall neatly into stocks, bonds, or real estate. They often promise high returns—or low correlation to traditional markets—but come with complexity.

What You Might Own:

- Commodities (gold, oil, agricultural products)
- Private equity (ownership in private companies)
- Venture capital (early-stage investing)
- Cryptocurrency (blockchain-based assets)
- Art, collectibles, wine, watches, etc.

Why They Matter:

- Offer potential diversification from stocks/bonds
- May offer high returns or hedge against inflation

How to Invest:

- Direct investments (if you qualify)
- ETFs or mutual funds with exposure to these assets
- Specialist platforms (e.g., Coinbase, AngelList)

Engineering Analogy:

Alternatives are prototype materials. Intriguing. Powerful. Volatile. Use with care and only after the core structure is sound.

EVALUATING TRADE-OFFS: THE ENGINEER'S DECISION TABLE

Return vs. Risk: Stocks offer growth. Bonds offer safety. Real estate sits somewhere in between. Alternatives? High variance.

Liquidity: Stocks and bonds can be sold fast. Real estate? Not so much. Alternatives vary wildly.

Tax Efficiency: Bonds generate income taxed at ordinary rates. Stocks may offer capital gains treatment. Real estate offers depreciation. Alternatives are unpredictable.

Effort and Complexity: Stocks and bonds via index funds = low effort. Real estate = higher involvement. Alternatives = requires niche knowledge.

BUILDING A SYSTEM WITH MULTIPLE MATERIALS

You wouldn't design a skyscraper with only concrete. Diversification isn't just a safety net. It's a structural requirement.

Sample Allocations:

Aggressive (under 35):

- 80% Stocks
- 10% Bonds
- 5% REITs
- 5% Alternatives

Balanced (35–55):

- 60% Stocks
- 30% Bonds
- 5% REITs
- 5% Alternatives

Conservative (55+):

- 40% Stocks
- 40% Bonds
- 10% REITs
- 10% Cash/Alternatives

Match your time horizon and volatility tolerance—not someone else's.

CASE STUDIES: ENGINEERS IN THE WILD

Case 1: Young Software Engineer, Age 25

- All in on Roth IRA with Total Stock Market ETF
- 401(k) invested in 90% equity target-date fund
- REITs in brokerage for tax-efficiency

Case 2: Civil Engineer, Age 40

- 401(k) in 70/30 stock/bond allocation
- Owns duplex generating $1,200/mo after expenses
- Uses cryptocurrency at 3% of total portfolio for speculative exposure

Case 3: Systems Engineer, Age 58

- 50/40/10 split (stocks/bonds/real estate)
- Regularly rebalances through automatic contributions
- Planning to annuitize part of the portfolio for retirement cash flow

ACTION STEPS

1. Identify your current allocation across the four asset classes
2. Match your allocation to your financial goals and timeframes
3. Use low-cost index funds for exposure to stocks/bonds
4. Evaluate real estate based on effort, leverage, and liquidity tolerance
5. Limit alternatives to less than 10% unless you're an expert
6. Rebalance annually using a spreadsheet, advisor, or target-date fund

A MOMENT OF ENCOURAGEMENT

You are not behind. You are not too late. You don't need to know everything about every asset to build wealth.

You just need to understand:

- What each piece of the system does
- Where it fits in your overall plan
- When to leave it alone and let it work

You're more capable than you think. You've designed bridges. Products. Code. Systems. Now you're designing freedom.

THE TAKEAWAY

Stocks are your growth engine. Bonds are your shock absorbers. Real estate is your slow-moving, income-producing platform. Alternatives are your experiments—if and only if your foundation is already strong.

This isn't just theory. It's architecture for your future.

FINAL NOTE

This book isn't just about money. It's about clarity. Control. Long-term thinking. And intentional decision-making.

Whether you want to retire early, build passive income, or leave a legacy, your asset choices are the bricks and beams of that structure.

Make them wisely. Engineer them intentionally. And revise when needed.

That's what resilient systems do. And that's exactly what you're building.

Chapter 15: Engineering Asset Allocation and Rebalancing

If you've ever designed a load-bearing structure, optimized a codebase, or calibrated a control system, then you already understand the fundamentals behind asset allocation and rebalancing—even if you've never applied them to your finances.

This chapter is about transforming that technical mindset into a financial advantage.

You're going to learn how to strategically assign different parts of your wealth to different functions—growth, stability, liquidity—and how to keep that system performing through market volatility, life changes, and emotional swings.

Because let's be clear: an investment portfolio isn't just something you *have*. It's something you *build*—intentionally, systematically, and iteratively. Just like any complex engineering system.

What Is Asset Allocation?

Asset allocation is the percentage breakdown of your investments across different asset classes—typically stocks, bonds, real estate, cash, and alternatives.

The goal? Maximize return *for your level of acceptable risk*.

Think of your portfolio like a structure. Stocks are your load-bearing beams—strong, but volatile. Bonds are your cross-bracing—less glamorous, but essential for stability. Real estate and alternatives are your secondary systems. And cash? That's your shock absorber and emergency reserve.

Why It Matters More Than Stock Picking

Academic studies show that asset allocation—not the individual securities you pick—is responsible for 90% of your portfolio's long-term performance.

In other words, how you structure your portfolio matters more than what you fill it with.

Core Principles of Asset Allocation

1. Time Horizon

- Longer time horizon = more stocks
- Shorter time horizon = more bonds and cash

Example: If you're saving for retirement 30 years away, stocks should dominate. If you're retiring in 5 years, bonds and cash will take on a larger role.

2. Risk Tolerance

- High tolerance = more volatile assets (stocks)
- Low tolerance = stable assets (bonds, cash)

This is emotional and behavioral. Don't guess—test yourself during market drops.

3. Goals and Liquidity Needs

Different goals demand different allocations. You wouldn't use high-volatility assets to fund next year's down payment.

Match your assets to their job:

- Growth = Stocks
- Income = Bonds
- Stability = Cash
- Inflation hedge = Real estate, TIPS
- Optionality/longshots = Alternatives

Sample Allocations

There's no one-size-fits-all, but here are some logical starting points:

Aggressive (20s–30s)

- 90% stocks (U.S. + international)
- 10% bonds

Balanced (40s–50s)

- 70% stocks
- 25% bonds
- 5% real estate or alternatives

Conservative (60+)

- 50% stocks
- 40% bonds
- 10% cash and real estate

Remember: these are models. You are the architect.

The Rebalancing Imperative

Asset allocation is a plan. Rebalancing is how you keep it on track.

As markets move, your allocation drifts. Left unchecked, risk builds up where you didn't intend.

What Rebalancing Does:

- Forces you to buy low and sell high
- Maintains intended risk exposure
- Prevents emotion-driven decisions

How Often?

- **Annually** is sufficient for most engineers
- **Semi-annually** for high-income/high-volatility portfolios
- **Threshold-based**: Rebalance when any asset class drifts >5% from target

How to Do It:

- Log into your brokerage or retirement account
- Check current percentages vs. target
- Sell over-allocated assets, buy under-allocated ones

Or...

- Use **new contributions** to rebalance without selling

Tax-Smart Rebalancing

In taxable accounts:

- Minimize capital gains by using new money to rebalance
- Harvest losses to offset gains when possible

In tax-advantaged accounts (401k, IRA):

- Rebalancing is frictionless—no tax hit
- Ideal place to house your rebalancing activity

Engineering the Rebalancing Schedule

Make it a process—not a reaction.

Create a Rebalancing Protocol:

1. Set a calendar reminder (once/year, same time every year)
2. Review current allocation vs. targets
3. Decide whether to rebalance via contributions or trades
4. Document what changed and why
5. Move on—don't tinker until next cycle

Common Allocation and Rebalancing Mistakes

1. Setting It and Forgetting It—Forever

Markets move. You change. A system that worked five years ago might now be misaligned.

2. Reacting Emotionally

You wouldn't scrap a bridge design because of a gusty day. Don't abandon your portfolio plan during market drops.

3. Chasing Performance

Don't overweight what's recently performed well. That's not rebalancing—it's gambling.

4. Ignoring Correlations

If all your funds drop at once, they might not be as diversified as you think. Make sure your stocks, bonds, and alternatives aren't all riding the same wave.

5. Overcomplicating It

You don't need 12 asset classes. You need clarity, simplicity, and systems.

Real-World Engineering Examples

Software Engineer, Age 26

- 90/10 stock/bond mix in Roth IRA
- Rebalances once per year using new contributions

Civil Engineer, Age 42

- 70/30 portfolio in 401(k) and brokerage
- Uses Excel model to rebalance quarterly
- Has 5% REIT exposure for diversification

Mechanical Engineer, Age 58

- 50/40/10 split (stocks/bonds/cash)
- Rebalances twice/year
- Uses bond ladder for near-term retirement income

Action Steps

1. Define your risk tolerance and time horizon
2. Choose an asset allocation model that aligns with your goals
3. Implement it using low-cost index funds or ETFs
4. Set a rebalancing date and stick to it
5. Automate new contributions to favor underweighted assets
6. Review yearly and adjust only if goals change

A Moment of Encouragement

You don't need a finance degree to build a resilient portfolio. You need a plan. You need discipline. You need a process.

You've already mastered this in your career. Now it's time to apply it to your wealth.

You are more capable than you think.

The Takeaway

Asset allocation isn't about beating the market. It's about aligning your resources with your values, timelines, and needs.

Rebalancing isn't about timing. It's about maintenance. Calibration. Engineering your financial system to perform over decades—not days.

When you allocate wisely and rebalance regularly, you create a portfolio that is:

- Built for the long haul

- Resilient under stress
- Aligned with who you are and what you want

You're not guessing. You're modeling. You're managing risk with structure—not superstition.

Final Note

This book isn't just about money. It's about:

- Treating your financial life like the complex, vital system it is
- Designing your portfolio with the same care you bring to your work
- Building wealth that outlasts your job, career, or industry

When you allocate well and rebalance with intention, you're not just investing. You're engineering freedom.

Stay the course. Tweak the system. And trust the process.

That's how engineers build wealth.

Part IV: Early Career Playbook – The First 10 Years

Your first decade in the workforce sets the tone for the rest of your financial life—and most engineers don't realize just how much leverage they have in these years. Part IV is your operating manual for building momentum, confidence, and clarity during this critical window.

Whether you're just out of school or already a few years into your career, this section will help you avoid the most common money traps young professionals face—like lifestyle creep, overcommitting to debt, or neglecting investments. You'll learn how to decode your paycheck, maximize your employer benefits, choose the right budget system, and begin investing like a pro without needing a finance degree. From paying down student loans to deciding whether to rent or buy, these chapters give you clear frameworks, engineer-specific examples, and actionable steps to take right now—not five years from now.

More than anything, this section is about building systems. Systems to help you automate progress, adapt to career changes, and establish a strong foundation before life gets more complicated.

The sooner you get this right, the more your money will work for you—freeing up your time, expanding your options, and setting you up for decades of compounding success.

Chapter 16: Choosing Between 401(k), Roth 401(k), and IRA

You're finally making good money. You want to start saving for retirement. You keep hearing about 401(k)s, Roth IRAs, traditional IRAs, and Roth 401(k)s.

But which one should you choose?

Welcome to one of the most pivotal decisions in your financial journey—and one of the most misunderstood. This chapter will walk you through it with precision, structure, and clarity. Like an engineer.

We're going to unpack the logic behind these retirement accounts so you can make a decision that aligns with your income, tax bracket, career trajectory, and long-term goals. No jargon. No fluff. Just clean architecture.

What Are These Accounts, Really?

Think of retirement accounts as different *containers*. The investments inside—stocks, bonds, index funds—can be similar across all of them. What changes is the **tax treatment** and **rules for access**.

Let's define the key players:

- **401(k)**: A tax-deferred retirement account offered by your employer.
- **Roth 401(k)**: A post-tax version of the 401(k).
- **Traditional IRA**: An individual retirement account with pre-tax contributions (if you qualify).

- **Roth IRA**: An individual retirement account where you contribute post-tax money.

The difference boils down to **when you pay taxes**:

- **Traditional 401(k) / IRA**: Pay taxes *later* when you withdraw.
- **Roth 401(k) / Roth IRA**: Pay taxes *now*, but withdrawals are tax-free later.

The 401(k): The Employer Power Tool

Key Features:

- Offered by your employer
- Contributions are pre-tax (Traditional) or post-tax (Roth)
- 2025 Contribution limit: $23,000 (under 50)
- Employer match does not count toward your limit
- Grows tax-deferred (Traditional) or tax-free (Roth)

Pros:

- High contribution limits
- Automatic payroll deductions
- Employer match = free money
- Loan options (in some cases)

Cons:

- Limited investment options (usually mutual funds only)
- Early withdrawal penalties (before age 59½)
- Required Minimum Distributions (RMDs) at age 73 (Traditional only)

Use If:

- Your employer offers a match
- You're a high earner in your peak tax years (Traditional)
- You expect to be in a higher bracket later (Roth)

The Roth 401(k): Pay Now, Reap Later

Key Features:

- Same plan structure as a 401(k)
- Funded with after-tax dollars
- Withdrawals in retirement are tax-free
- Same contribution limit as Traditional 401(k)

Pros:

- Tax-free growth AND withdrawals
- No income limits for contributions
- Best of both worlds: employer match goes into Traditional 401(k), you control your portion

Cons:

- Contributions reduce take-home pay now
- RMDs still apply (but can be avoided by rolling into a Roth IRA)

Use If:

- You're early in your career and in a low tax bracket
- You want tax-free income in retirement
- You're trying to hedge future tax hikes

The Traditional IRA: The DIY Retirement Shelter

Key Features:

- Individual account (not tied to employer)
- Contributions are tax-deductible (if eligible)
- Lower contribution limit: $7,000 in 2025
- Income limits apply for deduction eligibility

Pros:

- Tax-deferred growth
- Flexibility in investment choices (ETFs, stocks, etc.)
- Good if no employer plan exists

Cons:

- Lower contribution limits
- Deductibility phases out with higher income
- RMDs still apply

Use If:

- You don't have a 401(k)
- You're below the income deduction limits
- You want a simple way to reduce taxable income

The Roth IRA: The Quiet Compounding Machine

Key Features:

- Contributions are post-tax
- Earnings grow and withdraw tax-free
- 2025 limit: $7,000
- Income eligibility phases out above $161,000 (single), $240,000 (married)

Pros:

- No taxes in retirement
- No RMDs ever
- Contributions (not earnings) can be withdrawn at any time penalty-free

Cons:

- Contribution limits are low
- High earners may not qualify
- Requires discipline to avoid raiding the account early

Use If:

- You're early in your career
- You want a flexible emergency backup
- You plan to have significant income in retirement

The Backdoor Roth IRA: The Engineer's Loophole

High-income earners can't contribute directly to a Roth IRA, but there's a workaround:

1. Contribute to a **non-deductible Traditional IRA**
2. Convert it to a Roth IRA (paying little or no tax if done right)

This only works cleanly if you don't have other pre-tax IRA balances due to the **pro-rata rule**.

Consult a CPA before executing this.

How to Choose: Build a Decision Tree

Step 1: Do You Have a 401(k)?

- If yes: contribute at least enough to get the **full employer match**

Step 2: Traditional vs. Roth 401(k)?

- Low income now = Roth 401(k)
- High income now = Traditional 401(k)

Step 3: Can You Contribute to a Roth IRA?

- If under income limit, max it out
- If over limit, consider backdoor Roth

Step 4: Already maxed out 401(k) + IRA?

- Open a taxable brokerage account and invest there
- Use tax-efficient index funds or ETFs

Real-World Engineer Examples

Software Engineer, Age 24

- Roth 401(k) at work (low current tax bracket)
- Maxing Roth IRA as well

Civil Engineer, Age 35

- Traditional 401(k) + Backdoor Roth IRA annually
- Goal: tax diversification for retirement

Mechanical Engineer, Age 50

- Maxing Traditional 401(k) + catch-up contributions
- Evaluating Roth conversions before retirement

Action Steps

1. Log into your retirement plan portal and review your options
2. Check whether you're contributing to Roth or Traditional 401(k)
3. Run a rough tax estimate (use a free calculator or meet with a tax pro)
4. Open a Roth IRA or Traditional IRA if eligible
5. Set up automatic contributions monthly
6. Revisit annually or when your income shifts

A Moment of Encouragement

You don't have to master all the tax code. You just need to understand the levers:

- Pre-tax vs. after-tax
- Growth now vs. flexibility later
- Income limits and contribution thresholds

You're more capable than you think.

You already know how to optimize under constraints. You've worked within budget, time, and resource limits before. Now you're applying those same skills to your wealth.

The Takeaway

Your 401(k), Roth IRA, or Traditional IRA isn't just a savings plan. It's a decision engine. It's a tax tool. It's a structural beam in your future financial home.

Make it intentional. Make it automatic. And make it personal.

Final Note

This chapter wasn't about picking "the best" account. It was about designing the *right system for you*—based on your income, age, goals, and evolving life circumstances.

Whether you choose a Roth or Traditional path, what matters most is that you're *on the path*.

Stay disciplined. Stay curious. And keep optimizing.

Because you're not just contributing to a retirement account. You're engineering your future.

Chapter 17: How to Prioritize Saving vs. Investing vs. Paying Down Debt

This is one of the biggest balancing acts you'll face in your financial life.

And it shows up early.

You're earning more than you ever have. But now you have decisions to make.

Do you build a savings cushion? Do you start investing aggressively? Do you tackle that student loan, auto loan, or credit card debt?

If you're like most engineers, you want to find the mathematically optimal path. But this decision isn't just about math—it's also about emotion, behavior, and momentum.

This chapter will help you break it down logically, systemically, and with the long-term view in mind. You'll walk away knowing how to evaluate trade-offs, build a prioritization model, and confidently act—even when the choices feel murky.

Understand the Difference: Definitions First

Saving means setting aside cash for short-term needs, emergencies, or upcoming expenses. **Investing** means putting money into assets (stocks, bonds, etc.) that grow over time with some level of risk. **Paying down debt** means eliminating past obligations that carry interest.

Each of these has a role. None of them are bad. But not all of them should get your *first dollar*.

Create a Priority Flowchart

You don't need a rigid rulebook—you need a flowchart that evolves as your life does.

Start here:

Step 1: Build a Starter Emergency Fund

- Goal: $1,000 to $2,000 minimum
- Why? To prevent you from going further into debt when life hits

Step 2: Contribute to 401(k) up to Employer Match

- That's 100% return on your contribution—guaranteed

Step 3: Pay Off High-Interest Debt

- Anything above 7% interest is usually higher than your investment return
- Attack credit cards, personal loans, and bad car loans

Step 4: Build Full Emergency Fund

- Target: 3 to 6 months of expenses
- Store in a high-yield savings account or money market fund

Step 5: Max Out Roth IRA or Traditional IRA

- Tax-advantaged growth is powerful
- Max in 2025: $7,000

Step 6: Pay Down Moderate-Interest Debt

- Student loans, auto loans in 4–7% range
- Balance payoff with beginning to invest

Step 7: Invest in Taxable Brokerage Account

- Index funds, ETFs, long-term compounding

Step 8: Pay Down Low-Interest Debt

- Mortgage or student loans < 4%
- This becomes a values-based decision

Pros and Cons of Each Option

Saving:

Pros:

- Liquidity
- Safety
- Psychological security

Cons:

- Low returns
- Loses value to inflation over time

Investing:

Pros:

- Long-term wealth builder
- Compounding gains
- Tax-advantaged options

Cons:

- Market volatility
- Not liquid for emergencies

Paying Down Debt:

Pros:

- Guaranteed return (equal to interest rate)
- Reduces monthly obligations
- Improves credit score

Cons:

- Opportunity cost if investments outperform
- Once paid, funds are no longer liquid

The Engineer's Optimization Model

Let's say you have $1,000/month to allocate. How do you split it? Start with this three-bucket framework:

- **Security (savings)**: Until you hit 3–6 months
- **Growth (investing)**: Once employer match is secured

- **Efficiency (debt paydown)**: Based on interest rate

You can use Excel to model this with variables:

- Debt balance and interest rate
- Expected market return
- Emergency fund needs
- Monthly cash flow available

Real-World Examples

Case 1: Software Engineer, Age 25

- $4,000 credit card debt at 22%
- $1,200 in savings
- Employer matches 3% on 401(k)

Plan:

- Emergency fund to $2,000
- 401(k) to match
- Aggressively pay down credit card

Case 2: Civil Engineer, Age 35

- $12,000 in student loans at 5.5%
- $20,000 in savings
- Not investing at all

Plan:

- Emergency fund is done
- Begin maxing Roth IRA

- Pay off student loans steadily over 3–5 years

Case 3: Mechanical Engineer, Age 45

- Mortgage at 3.2%
- Maxing 401(k)
- Wants to retire at 55

Plan:

- Keep low-rate mortgage
- Open brokerage account
- Explore Roth conversions

Behavioral Traps to Avoid

1. **Analysis Paralysis:** Don't wait for the perfect spreadsheet. Build momentum.
2. **All-or-Nothing Thinking:** You can split between saving, investing, and debt. It's not binary.
3. **Ignoring Liquidity:** Don't invest everything and leave yourself cashless. Emergencies happen.
4. **Neglecting Employer Match:** Never leave free money on the table.
5. **Comparing to Friends:** Your plan isn't theirs. Customize based on your numbers.

Action Steps

1. Inventory your savings, debt balances, interest rates, and income
2. Use the flowchart above to identify your next best step
3. Automate contributions to savings and investing
4. Create a debt payoff plan and automate it if possible
5. Set a calendar reminder to review progress every 6 months

A Moment of Encouragement

You don't need to have it all figured out.

But you do need to move.

Your first $100 invested. Your first $1,000 saved. Your last credit card balance paid in full.

These are all wins. And they compound.

You're not just allocating money. You're engineering freedom.

You are more capable than you think.

The Takeaway

You don't have to choose between saving, investing, and paying off debt forever. You prioritize, sequence, automate, and adjust.

And then you let the system work.

Because that's what smart engineers do.

Final Note

This isn't about squeezing every drop of return. It's about:

- Having cash when you need it
- Growing wealth while you work
- Freeing yourself from debt that drains you

You're not picking between good and bad. You're building a financial structure that reflects your life.

With every payment, every contribution, and every decision, you're not just reacting.

You're designing.

And that's what separates the overwhelmed from the financially free.

Chapter 18: Optimizing Health Savings Accounts (HSA) and FSAs

Let's talk about one of the most underused—and underrated—tools in your financial toolbox: the Health Savings Account (HSA).

And let's also break down its cousin: the Flexible Spending Account (FSA).

If you're an engineer who appreciates optimization, tax efficiency, and getting the most out of every dollar—you're going to love this chapter.

Because HSAs and FSAs are more than just "benefits paperwork." They're systems. With rules. Leverage. And long-term potential.

Done right, they can help you lower your taxable income, cover out-of-pocket healthcare expenses tax-free, and even build wealth for retirement.

What is an HSA?

A Health Savings Account (HSA) is a tax-advantaged account available to people who are enrolled in a **High Deductible Health Plan (HDHP).**

Think of an HSA as a **triple-tax-advantaged** account:

1. You contribute pre-tax dollars
2. The money grows tax-free
3. Withdrawals are tax-free when used for qualified medical expenses

This is as close to a "perfect" tax structure as exists in U.S. financial planning.

2025 HSA Contribution Limits:

- Individual: $4,300
- Family: $8,650
- Additional $1,000 catch-up if you're 55+

What is an FSA?

A Flexible Spending Account (FSA) is an employer-sponsored account that lets you contribute **pre-tax dollars** for health care or dependent care expenses.

Unlike the HSA, you don't need to be on an HDHP to qualify.

But there's a catch: most FSAs operate on a **use-it-or-lose-it** model. That means any money you don't use by the end of the plan year (or grace period) is forfeited.

2025 FSA Contribution Limits:

- Health Care FSA: $3,200
- Dependent Care FSA: $5,000 (married filing jointly)

HSA vs. FSA: Key Differences

Feature HSA FSA

Eligibility

Must have HDHP

Employer plan, no HDHP required

Contribution Limits

Higher

Lower

Rollover

Yes (indefinite)

Usually no (grace period or $640 rollover)

Portability
You own it
Tied to employer
Investment Option
Yes
Rarely
Catch-Up Contributions
Yes (55+)
No

Why the HSA is a Supercharged Tool

You don't have to use your HSA every year. That's the beauty.

You can **pay out-of-pocket now**, let the account grow, and **reimburse yourself later**—years or even decades down the line.

That means you can invest your HSA like a retirement account.

And if you save your receipts, you can take a tax-free withdrawal at any point in the future, even for expenses you already paid.

That's flexibility. That's optimization. That's engineering your healthcare strategy.

Strategic Uses of HSAs

1. **Emergency Medical Fund:** Keep cash in the HSA, ready to cover surprise expenses tax-free.
2. **Investment Growth Account:** Treat it like a stealth retirement account and invest the balance.
3. **Tax Arbitrage Tool:** Contribute when in a high tax bracket, withdraw later tax-free.
4. **Long-Term Care Hedge:** Qualified long-term care expenses are HSA-eligible.
5. **Retirement Bridge:** After age 65, you can withdraw for non-medical reasons penalty-free (you just pay income tax—like a Traditional IRA).

Strategic Uses of FSAs

1. **Known Medical Expenses:** Schedule dental work, vision exams, or prescriptions around your FSA plan year.
2. **Childcare Support:** Use a Dependent Care FSA to pay daycare, preschool, or summer camp expenses with pre-tax dollars.
3. **Bridging Coverage Gaps:** FSAs work well when you don't qualify for an HSA or want short-term medical savings.

Engineer-Specific Scenarios

Scenario 1: 27-Year-Old Software Engineer

- Enrolled in HDHP
- No chronic conditions
- Minimal annual healthcare costs

Strategy: Max HSA, invest balance, pay out-of-pocket for routine visits
Scenario 2: 38-Year-Old Project Engineer with Kids

- Traditional PPO plan with Dependent Care FSA
- Annual childcare expenses $10,000+

Strategy: Max Dependent Care FSA, save $1,500+ in taxes
Scenario 3: 52-Year-Old Lead Mechanical Engineer

- HDHP participant
- Chronic joint pain + annual physical therapy costs

Strategy: Split HSA into cash and investments, reimburse self yearly

Common Mistakes Engineers Make

1. **Not choosing the HSA plan because of higher deductible.** You may pay more upfront—but the tax and investment benefits often outweigh it over time.
2. **Using the HSA like a checking account.** If you can afford to pay expenses out-of-pocket, let the HSA grow.
3. **Forgetting to save receipts.** Every copay, dental cleaning, or prescription can be reimbursed years later.
4. **Underfunding the FSA, then scrambling.** Estimate your expenses carefully, especially for planned procedures.
5. **Overfunding an FSA and losing money.** Better to be conservative unless you're certain about your healthcare usage.

Action Steps

1. Check if your employer offers an HSA or FSA option.
2. Review your past year's medical expenses.
3. Estimate upcoming healthcare costs and childcare needs.
4. Decide whether to use the HSA for immediate or long-term purposes.
5. Set up HSA investing if your balance is over $2,000 (threshold varies).
6. Save digital copies of all receipts in a secure folder.
7. Automate contributions through payroll, if available.

A Moment of Encouragement

You don't need to be a tax attorney or benefits specialist.

You just need to think like an engineer:

- Inputs
- Outputs
- Constraints
- Optimization

The HSA is one of the cleanest, most powerful systems available to you.

And the FSA, while more limited, can still create serious savings.

Every dollar you protect from taxes is a dollar that works for you—not against you.

You're more capable than you think.

The Takeaway

HSAs and FSAs aren't just acronyms on HR forms. They're strategic systems.

And when you understand the mechanics—the contribution limits, tax treatments, investment options—you unlock one of the most overlooked parts of financial planning.

You optimize today. You build security for tomorrow. You gain control.

And you do it all with the same mindset you bring to engineering: precision, structure, and long-term thinking.

Final Note

There will be years when healthcare costs spike—and years when they don't.

But your strategy can stay consistent:

- Maximize tax efficiency
- Invest where possible
- Be thoughtful with estimates
- Keep good records

You're not just covering copays and prescriptions.

You're engineering a system that protects your income, builds wealth, and gives you peace of mind.

And that's the smartest kind of engineering there is.

Chapter 20: Renting vs Buying – Engineering the Housing Decision

One of the biggest financial questions you'll face as an engineer isn't just about your salary, investments, or benefits—it's about where you live. More specifically, whether you should rent or buy your home. This decision can have six-figure implications over your lifetime.

And yet, too often, engineers default into home ownership without running the numbers. Or they rent forever out of fear or inertia.

This chapter is about using the same analytical mindset that makes you an excellent engineer to make one of life's most emotional and complex financial decisions.

Let's remove the emotion. Let's map the variables. Let's engineer a decision.

Why This Decision Matters

Housing isn't just a roof over your head—it's often your largest monthly expense, your biggest investment (or not), and your most emotional asset.

Whether you rent or buy affects:

- Your cash flow
- Your flexibility
- Your tax strategy

- Your investment strategy
- Your stress levels

You're not deciding between good and bad. You're deciding between two systems with different trade-offs.

Pros and Cons of Renting

Pros:

- Flexibility to move
- No maintenance costs
- Lower upfront costs (no down payment)
- Can invest the difference in the market
- No market risk on property value

Cons:

- Rent can increase annually
- No equity building
- Limited customization
- Subject to landlord rules or sudden changes

Pros and Cons of Buying

Pros:

- Build equity over time
- Mortgage payment can be fixed
- Tax deductions (mortgage interest, property taxes)
- Pride of ownership and stability
- Potential for appreciation

Cons:

- High upfront costs (down payment, closing costs)
- Maintenance and repairs are your responsibility
- Less flexibility to move
- Market risk (home value can drop)
- Transaction costs on both ends (buying and selling)

The Real Math Behind Renting vs Buying

Let's get into what most financial blogs oversimplify.

Buying isn't always better. Renting isn't always wasteful.

It depends on the **total cost of ownership** vs. the **total cost of renting adjusted for opportunity cost**.

What to Include in the Cost of Buying:

- Mortgage payment (principal + interest)
- Property taxes
- Homeowners insurance
- Maintenance (1% to 2% of home value annually)
- HOA fees (if applicable)
- Closing costs
- Opportunity cost of the down payment (i.e., what it could earn in the market)

What to Include in the Cost of Renting:

- Monthly rent
- Renters insurance
- Annual rent increases (typically 2% to 5%)
- Lost equity building (but gain flexibility)

Opportunity Cost:

If you rent and invest the difference between your rent and what it would cost to own (including all those hidden expenses), you might come out ahead.

This is what most people miss.

Engineers should love this problem because it can be modeled.

Build Your Housing Decision Model

Use a spreadsheet or tool like the NYT Rent vs. Buy calculator, and input:

- Home price
- Down payment
- Mortgage interest rate
- Property tax rate
- Maintenance estimate
- Expected years in the home
- Estimated annual appreciation
- Estimated annual rent increase
- Expected investment return (for opportunity cost)

Then run the numbers.

Time Horizon: The Ultimate Variable

The longer you stay in a home, the more buying tends to make sense.

Why? Because the high upfront costs of buying (agent commissions, loan fees, title insurance) get spread out over more years.

Rule of Thumb: If you won't stay at least 5–7 years, buying rarely makes financial sense.

Liquidity: Don't Go House Broke

Owning a home doesn't make you rich if it sucks all your liquidity. Many engineers overextend:

- 20% down on a $700K home = $140K
- Add closing costs = ~$20K
- Now you're down $160K, plus you owe $560K

What if your HVAC dies? Or you lose your job? Or the market dips? You need:

- Emergency fund (3–6 months minimum)
- Budget for maintenance
- Cushion for life events

Buying a home is not a substitute for financial security.

Behavioral Factors: What Engineers Often Overlook

1. Anchoring Bias

You saw your friend buy and now feel like you're behind. That's not a data point.

2. Sunk Cost Fallacy

Just because you spent $50K in renovations doesn't mean your home increased in value by that much.

3. Confirmation Bias

You read articles that support your decision, but ignore ones that challenge it.

4. Status Symbol Trap

Buying a house to "feel successful" can lead to overbuying.

Renting Isn't Throwing Money Away

You pay to live somewhere. Always.

With renting, you pay a landlord. With owning, you pay a bank, a tax assessor, an HOA, and a contractor.

Don't mistake cash flow for equity building.

It's only equity **if** the home appreciates and **if** you sell it.

Until then, it's a fixed location with a lot of responsibility.

Renting Isn't Always Cheaper

In some high-rent cities, buying actually makes more sense if you can do it with a reasonable down payment and plan to stay a while.

Every market is different. Run the math.

How Engineers Can Think About Housing

Design Your Life First

Where do you want to be for the next 5+ years?

What do you value more: flexibility or control?

Run the Model

Use a spreadsheet to calculate:

- Total 5-year cost of renting
- Total 5-year cost of buying
- Break-even appreciation rate
- After-tax benefit of deductions

Optimize the Variables

Can you rent in a walkable neighborhood for less and invest the difference?

Can you buy a smaller home in a lower-tax district and avoid overcommitting?

Reevaluate Annually

Life changes. So should your housing strategy.

Action Steps

1. List your goals: mobility, schools, equity building, lifestyle
2. Get prequalified to know your buying power
3. Run a rent vs. buy calculator for your area
4. Model the opportunity cost of your down payment
5. Ask: Can I afford this and still hit my savings/investment goals?
6. Talk to a financial advisor before making an offer

A Moment of Encouragement

You don't need to own to be financially successful. You don't need to rent forever to stay flexible.

You just need to make a decision rooted in math, not emotion.

You already have the tools. You already think in systems. Now you just need to apply them to your housing life.

The Takeaway

Renting vs. buying isn't a moral decision. It's not a status decision. It's a system decision.

Treat it like you would any design question:

- Gather data
- Model the system
- Define your constraints
- Optimize for outcomes

And when in doubt, choose what gives you the most **options**, the most **resilience**, and the most **peace of mind**.

That's engineering your financial life.

Final Note

Whether you rent or buy, your home is just one part of your plan.

Don't let it dominate your portfolio. Don't let it derail your liquidity. Don't let it distract you from the bigger picture.

You are not a house. You are a systems thinker, a problem-solver, and a builder of your future.

Act like it. Own your process. And build a life that works for you—not the other way around.

Part V: Strategic Career and Wealth Moves

Focuses on how engineers can align their financial decisions with the different stages of their career trajectory. This section isn't about technical certifications or job titles—it's about using your career as a powerful engine for long-term wealth creation. Whether you're negotiating your first offer, navigating promotions, changing industries, or considering side ventures, these chapters equip you with tools to evaluate risk, forecast income growth, and make strategic trade-offs. You'll learn how to view compensation holistically (salary, benefits, equity), how to optimize for both income and fulfillment, and how to shift from purely earning to leveraging your earnings for generational impact. This part of the book will show you how to treat your career as a portfolio—something you manage, iterate, and optimize over time.

Chapter 21: Salary Negotiation for Engineers – Maximizing Offers

Let's talk about one of the most pivotal financial moments in your engineering career: salary negotiation. Whether you're fresh out of college or 15 years into your profession, knowing how to evaluate, counter, and accept offers is one of the most financially impactful skills you can develop. Yet it's a skill rarely taught in engineering school—and even more rarely discussed at work.

For engineers who thrive on logic, data, and systems, approaching salary negotiation with structure will not only increase your compensation—it will empower you to better understand your market value and long-term potential. This chapter is designed to give you a framework. Not just for one negotiation, but for a lifetime of maximizing your income strategically.

Understanding Your Market Value

Market value isn't just what a company is willing to pay—it's a combination of your experience, skills, certifications, specialization, and geographic location. You must start here. Too many engineers accept their first offer without asking, researching, or benchmarking.

Action Step: Use platforms like Glassdoor, Levels.fyi, Blind, and LinkedIn Salary Insights to gather current compensation data. Don't rely on one source—triangulate.

Key Insight: Your market value is not static. It evolves as you gain project experience, earn promotions, learn new skills, or relocate.

The Psychology of Negotiation

Engineers often over-index on logic and under-appreciate psychology. The truth is, negotiation is both. If you fear being "greedy," think of negotiation as a calibration process—not confrontation.

Rule of Thumb: The first offer is often not the best offer. It's the beginning of the conversation.

Common Trap: Accepting too quickly out of fear they might rescind the offer. Most legitimate companies expect a counter.

Dissecting the Offer Letter

Before you negotiate, break the offer down into its parts:

- **Base salary**
- **Bonus (signing and/or performance)**
- **Equity (RSUs, ESPPs, options)**
- **Benefits (healthcare, HSA/FSA, PTO, 401(k) match, life insurance)**
- **Perks (relocation assistance, learning stipends, travel, work-from-home flexibility)**

Action Step: Assign each component a value—and consider your priorities.

Engineering the Counter-Offer

This is where many engineers get uncomfortable. Here's a structured approach:

1. **Express appreciation:** Always thank them for the offer.
2. **Reiterate your enthusiasm:** Make it clear you're genuinely interested.

3. **State your ask:** Use clear, concise language: "Based on market benchmarks and the scope of the role, I was hoping we could discuss a base closer to $X."
4. **Justify it:** Point to data, past experience, or higher competing offers if you have them.

Pro Tip: Don't negotiate over email alone. Set up a phone call or Zoom.

The Trade-Off Matrix

Engineers love systems. Use a trade-off matrix to evaluate:

- **Company prestige vs. role learning curve**
- **Salary vs. equity vs. lifestyle**
- **Short-term cash vs. long-term growth**
- **Tech stack vs. mentorship vs. location**

Case Study: Maria, a mechanical engineer, received two offers:

- Offer A: $95K base, great 401(k) match, poor work-life balance.
- Offer B: $88K base, no match, flexible remote policy.

Maria valued flexibility for her young family. She chose Offer B, knowing she could negotiate the base up to $90K and use the difference to fund her own IRA.

When to Walk Away

Sometimes, walking away is the smartest negotiation move. If a company won't budge, or if the total compensation is too far below market, or if their culture punishes people who ask for more—pay attention. You're not just negotiating pay. You're testing alignment.

Rule of Thumb: If the offer feels too low *and* their attitude about your counter feels dismissive, it might not be the right fit.

Special Considerations for Engineers

- **Government vs. private vs. startup compensation**
- **Cost-of-living adjustments**
- **Relocation and tax implications**
- **Dual-income household planning**
- **Equity-heavy packages and vesting schedules**

Tools and Spreadsheets

Build a simple spreadsheet to model scenarios:

- 3-year forecast of salary, equity vesting, and bonus projections
- Adjusted for taxes and cost of living
- Include out-of-pocket healthcare and childcare expenses

Salary Negotiation and Wealth Building

Every $5,000 you negotiate in base salary could be worth $100,000+ over a 30-year career due to compounding raises and retirement contributions.

Formula: Salary x (annual raise %) x (employer retirement match %) x (years worked)

Final Encouragement

You are not just an engineer. You are a wealth-builder.

Negotiating isn't selfish—it's strategic. You don't need to be aggressive. Just prepared. Practice. Use data. Lead with clarity and confidence.

Remember: Engineers design bridges, systems, and machines. You can design your financial life with the same intentionality. Negotiation is one of the first and most powerful tools in that blueprint.

Takeaway: The smartest engineers don't just accept offers. They assess, model, counter, and iterate.

Chapter 22: Certifications, Graduate Degrees, and ROI

Let's get one thing clear from the beginning: not every professional certification or advanced degree automatically adds value to your career. As an engineer, you are conditioned to trust systems, accreditation, and credentials. But when it comes to your financial life, not every letter after your name translates into dollars in your pocket or freedom in your future.

This chapter is about demystifying the decision-making process behind graduate school and professional certifications. Whether you're weighing the value of an MBA, an MS in a technical field, a PE license, PMP, Six Sigma certification, or a PhD, you need to apply the same logic you would to any engineering project: clear requirements, expected outputs, resource allocation, ROI projections, and risk assessment.

We'll walk through:

- What credentials engineers typically pursue
- Why certain certifications carry more weight in some industries than others
- How to calculate the return on investment for grad school or a certification
- The opportunity cost of time, money, and energy spent in school vs. the workplace
- Scenarios where the payoff justifies the price—and where it doesn't

- And how to make the decision not just based on prestige, but purpose

Because here's the truth: You don't need more credentials to feel worthy. You need a better system to evaluate the role those credentials play in your long-term career and financial plans. You're not just a student of engineering. You're a builder of your own economic life.

In this chapter, we'll also dig into real stories of engineers who:

- Increased their income dramatically by earning a strategic certification
- Took on grad school debt and regretted it
- Used employer-sponsored tuition reimbursement as a way to stack credentials without financial strain
- Delayed promotions because they thought they needed a degree they didn't

Every decision has trade-offs. But if you learn how to model the value of credentials like an engineer, you can avoid defaulting into a path just because everyone else is on it. You can design your learning strategy the way you would design a product: with purpose, performance benchmarks, and smart constraints.

By the end of this chapter, you won't just know what options are available to you. You'll know how to think about them.

Because the most powerful credential isn't on your business card.

It's your ability to think critically, plan strategically, and act decisively in pursuit of a better financial future.

Chapter 23: The Financial Impact of Changing Jobs

Let's talk about the moment you get the offer.

You've interviewed, negotiated, and gotten the call: "We're thrilled to offer you the position." Maybe it's more money. Maybe it's a better title. Maybe it's remote. Maybe it's closer to your family or the kind of work you've always wanted to do. Whatever the reason, you're seriously considering changing jobs.

Now what?

Changing jobs isn't just a career decision—it's a financial system disruption. Whether you're a 26-year-old software engineer jumping startups, a 41-year-old civil engineer moving into management, or a 58-year-old mechanical engineer transitioning into pre-retirement consulting, the financial implications ripple far beyond the paycheck.

This chapter is about helping you make a job change with eyes wide open.

It's about more than salary. It's about benefits, equity, timing, taxes, opportunity cost, lifestyle impact, and long-term wealth strategy.

Let's break it down, engineer-style.

Understanding the Total Compensation Package

First: don't get hypnotized by salary.

Base pay is only one piece of your compensation system. A true financial analysis must include:

- Base Salary

- Annual Bonus
- Signing Bonus
- Stock Options or RSUs
- 401(k) Match
- Insurance Coverage (Health, Dental, Vision, Life, Disability)
- Paid Time Off
- Tuition Reimbursement or Continuing Education
- Remote Work Allowance or Commute Costs
- Severance Structure

Action Step: Build a compensation comparison spreadsheet. Line by line. Apples to apples. Total value, not just base pay.

Real-World Example:

Jared, a mid-level electrical engineer, was offered a new job with a $15,000 higher salary. But after analyzing benefits, he realized his old job had a 6% 401(k) match, better health insurance, and a year-end bonus. The net difference? Only $3,000. He negotiated a signing bonus and accepted—but didn't let base pay blind him.

Hidden Costs of Job Transitions

Every job change has friction costs. You might face:

- Unused PTO forfeited
- Loss of unvested equity
- Delays in 401(k) eligibility (some companies impose a 6- to 12-month wait)
- Gaps in health insurance coverage
- Relocation expenses
- Licensing, certification, or professional dues
- Lower HSA contributions or no FSA options

Action Step: Ask for a transition support package. Some employers will cover COBRA costs, pay relocation, or front-load PTO.

Timing Matters—Especially With Taxes

Job changes impact your tax picture more than most realize.

Let's say you receive:

- A signing bonus
- A payout for unused vacation
- A year-end bonus from your old employer

That's a lot of lump-sum income in one year.

Implications:

- Pushes you into a higher marginal tax bracket
- Reduces eligibility for certain deductions or credits
- May trigger phase-outs on student loan interest deductions or Roth IRA contributions

Action Step: Work with a tax advisor to model income under both jobs. Time your start date or bonuses if possible to spread income across tax years.

How to Handle Your Old 401(k)

When you leave a job, you've got four main options for your retirement plan:

1. Leave it with your former employer (if allowed)
2. Roll it into your new employer's plan
3. Roll it into an IRA
4. Cash it out (rarely recommended due to penalties and taxes)

Pros of leaving it:

- Simplicity if you like the plan

Pros of rolling it over:

- Consolidation, better investment options, more control

Cons of cashing out:

- Immediate tax hit
- 10% penalty if under 59½
- Loss of compounding potential

Action Step: Compare fees and fund choices in old vs. new plans. Make a decision within 60 days to avoid complications.

Health Insurance Gaps and Options

If there's a delay between jobs, you may go without employer-sponsored health insurance. Options include:

- COBRA (keep old plan, pay full premium + 2% fee)
- Spouse's plan (if available)
- ACA marketplace coverage
- Short-term health insurance (temporary coverage, fewer benefits)

Scenario:

You leave your job on March 15 and start your new one on May 1. That's six weeks uncovered. One ER visit could cost thousands.

Action Step: Don't wing it. Know your options and costs before giving notice.

Managing RSUs, ISOs, and ESPPs When You Leave

If you've received equity compensation, changing jobs gets tricky.

Restricted Stock Units (RSUs):

- Unvested RSUs are usually forfeited
- Vested RSUs may be taxed upon delivery

Incentive Stock Options (ISOs):

- 90-day window to exercise after termination
- May lose favorable tax treatment if not exercised correctly

Employee Stock Purchase Plans (ESPPs):

- Check whether you'll receive prorated shares
- Understand taxation on disqualifying dispositions

Action Step: Before you resign, talk to HR or the equity administrator. Get documentation. Run the numbers with a tax pro.

Evaluating Job Changes Through the Lens of FIRE

If you're on a path to Financial Independence, Retire Early (FIRE), every job move matters.

Ask:

- Does this accelerate or delay my FIRE date?
- Does it raise or lower my annual expenses?
- Will it give me more time to build side income or invest?

Real-World Example:

Luis, a 34-year-old software engineer, took a remote job that paid $10K less but allowed him to move to a lower-cost state, cut commuting expenses, and start a YouTube channel. Net effect? He saved more, not less.

Action Step: Update your FIRE projection spreadsheet. Adjust for new salary, expenses, and savings rate.

Lifestyle and Opportunity Cost

Money matters—but so does energy.

Changing jobs can:

- Reduce or increase commute time
- Change how much energy you have at night (for family or side hustles)
- Affect your mental health and productivity
- Shift your networking opportunities

You're not just choosing a paycheck. You're choosing a rhythm.

Scenario:

Vanessa took a job that paid $20K more but required 20% travel. After six months, she realized she missed too many family moments. The money didn't feel worth it.

Action Step: Assign dollar values to non-monetary benefits (e.g., remote work, flexible hours, team culture). Compare offers on more than money.

Negotiating with the Future in Mind

If you're changing jobs, this is your leverage moment. Don't waste it.

Things to negotiate beyond salary:

- Signing bonus
- PTO matching (e.g., if you had 4 weeks at old job, ask to match)
- Work-from-home flexibility
- Professional development budget
- 401(k) eligibility timeline

Real-World Tip:

Don't ask, "Can you match this?"

Instead ask, "What can we do to close the gap on XYZ?"

Action Step: Prepare a script. Practice it. Frame everything in terms of value you bring and problems you'll solve.

Transitioning Smoothly: Financial Checklist

Before giving notice:

- Confirm health insurance end date
- Max out HSA or FSA if possible
- Capture final 401(k) contributions
- Use any remaining education reimbursement
- Secure any bonus or vesting payouts

After accepting:

- Set up direct deposit and tax withholdings
- Reevaluate withholdings on new W-4
- Opt into benefits ASAP
- Start 401(k) contributions immediately
- Update your budget and automate savings

Action Step: Create a "job change transition checklist" to track all action items.

Encouragement

You're more capable than you think.

A job change can feel overwhelming—but you've debugged tougher systems. You've analyzed tradeoffs in harder decisions.

Just approach it like an engineer:

- Gather data
- Model the outcomes
- Optimize for clarity, not perfection

The smartest engineers don't jump jobs impulsively. They shift strategically.

Takeaways

- Evaluate total comp, not just salary
- Anticipate timing, taxes, and hidden costs
- Know your equity implications and rollover options
- Use job changes to optimize your lifestyle, not just your income
- Plan the transition with as much rigor as you'd plan a project rollout

Final Reminder

Changing jobs isn't just about chasing more money. It's about aligning your work, your life, and your finances.

Engineer your next move.

With precision.

With intention.

With clarity.

Chapter 24: Consulting, Freelancing, and Side Projects

Let's talk about something that most engineers think about at some point in their careers: consulting, freelancing, and launching side projects. Whether you're a 24-year-old software engineer intrigued by the startup scene, a 35-year-old civil engineer looking to pick up freelance work on the weekends, or a 60-year-old mechanical engineer who's ready to consult part-time in retirement, side work isn't just about extra income. It's about autonomy, opportunity, and options.

It's also a financial minefield if you're not thoughtful.

This chapter will walk you through how to think about side gigs like a systems problem: with clarity, logic, strategy, and long-term thinking.

We'll go deep into:

- The differences between consulting, freelancing, and passion projects
- How to evaluate whether a side income stream fits your goals
- The tax, legal, and financial implications of moonlighting
- How to set your rates, track income, and manage cash flow
- How to scale a side hustle without wrecking your W-2 job
- How to protect your intellectual property and avoid common legal traps
- When a side hustle becomes a business—and how to structure it properly
- How to prioritize energy, time, and bandwidth across multiple roles

We'll use a clean, structured, no-fluff format to make it easy to apply in real life. Because let's be honest: if you wanted vague motivational fluff, you'd be reading an Instagram quote, not a financial literacy book for engineers.

So let's build your freelance framework. Let's model your side hustle like an engineering project. Let's optimize for upside, reduce unnecessary risk, and design a plan that earns, scales, and serves your bigger financial life.

Chapter 25: Intellectual Property, Royalties, and Passive Income

Let's talk about building wealth beyond your W-2. If you're an engineer, you already think in systems. You build, iterate, optimize, and debug complex problems every day. Your mind is wired to look for efficiencies, leverage, and scalable outcomes. So what if I told you that there are ways to use those same engineering skills to build a financial system that pays you—even when you're not actively working? That's the power of intellectual property, royalties, and passive income.

This chapter isn't about get-rich-quick schemes or influencer gimmicks. It's about durable income streams that take planning, design, and in many cases, technical skill to execute. But once they're in place, they can reduce your financial dependence on your job, buffer your retirement timeline, and give you freedom to explore more meaningful work.

Let's dive in.

What Is Intellectual Property?

Intellectual Property (IP) refers to creations of the mind—things you invent, write, design, or code. The key difference from physical property is that IP isn't tangible, but it still has value and can be legally protected.

Types of Intellectual Property:

- Patents: Protect inventions. Think: A new type of circuit board, sensor, or piece of software with a novel algorithm.
- Trademarks: Protect brand identity. Think: Logos, product names, or

slogans tied to an engineering consultancy.
- Copyrights: Protect original works. Think: A textbook, blog, or CAD tutorial you created.
- Trade Secrets: Protect proprietary knowledge. Think: A unique engineering process or internal tool that gives a company an edge.

Engineers often create intellectual property without even realizing it. If you've written a whitepaper, designed a product, or built a system for your employer, chances are IP was involved. Understanding this is crucial—especially if you're considering side projects or entrepreneurship.

Ownership Matters

The first thing to know about IP is this: If you create it as part of your job, your employer likely owns it. Most employment contracts include an IP clause that assigns any inventions or innovations to the company—especially if you used company time or resources.

However, if you're working on something entirely separate, on your own time, with your own equipment, you may retain full ownership. But tread carefully. Even gray areas (like working on a side project on a company laptop) can cause issues.

Action Step: Review your employment agreement. If you're doing any outside work, get clarity on what your company considers its property.

Why Intellectual Property Can Be a Financial Asset

IP is valuable because it can generate income. Just like you might rent out a house or sell a product, you can license or sell your intellectual property to others. This is where royalties come in.

Royalties 101

Royalties are payments you receive for granting someone else the right to use your IP. These can be one-time fees, ongoing payments, or a percentage of sales. In engineering, royalty income might come from:

- Licensing your software library to another company
- Selling CAD templates or 3D models
- Publishing a book or course that gets purchased repeatedly

- Licensing a patent for a device or system you designed

These are scalable. Once created, they can be sold or licensed over and over—without trading time for money.

Real-World Example:

Meet Jason, a mechanical engineer who developed a unique mechanism for reducing vibration in small engines. He patented it. A small manufacturer licensed his patent and paid him $20,000 upfront plus $5 per unit sold. Over five years, he made over $150,000 in royalties—all while working his day job.

Or consider Priya, a software engineer who built a suite of Python tools for data visualization in her free time. She packaged them into a premium course and earned $40,000 in the first year alone.

This is passive income done right.

Understanding Passive Income

Let's demystify this term.

Passive income is money you earn with little ongoing effort. The keyword is "ongoing." It may require a lot of upfront work—writing, coding, designing—but once the system is built, it can run with minimal maintenance.

There are three main passive income models engineers should know:

1. Licensing Intellectual Property
2. Creating Digital Products (e.g. courses, books, templates)
3. Building Investment Income (e.g. dividends, real estate)

Let's break each down.

1. Licensing Intellectual Property
2. Already covered above, but the takeaway is this: If you've built something useful, others may want to use it. You can license that use while keeping ownership. This works well for:

- Software libraries
- Engineering models
- Algorithms
- Hardware designs

Pros:

- Scalable
- Low maintenance once set up
- Income potential increases with reach

Cons:

- Legal costs for patenting or contracts
- Can be hard to enforce without legal help

Action Step: If you have a marketable product or design, explore provisional patents or open-source + premium models.

1. Creating Digital Products
2. This is one of the most accessible forms of passive income for engineers.

Ideas include:

- Writing eBooks or guides on your specialty
- Creating video tutorials on MATLAB, Python, or AutoCAD
- Selling spreadsheets, design templates, or troubleshooting checklists
- Building an email course for junior engineers

Real Example:

Mark, a civil engineer, created a $49 course on structural load calculations. It took him three weekends. He promoted it via LinkedIn and a small email list. It made $2,000 in the first month and $1,200/month afterward.

The key is niching down—solve a specific problem for a specific audience.

Pros:

- High margins
- Can reach global audience
- Builds your brand

Cons:

- Time-intensive upfront
- Marketing matters (it won't sell itself)
- Risk of low sales if poorly positioned

Action Step: Make a list of the 10 questions junior engineers ask you most often. That's your digital product roadmap.

1. Investment Income
2. While not IP-related, it's worth covering.

Engineers often excel at long-term thinking, which makes them great candidates for building income-generating portfolios.

Types:

- Dividends from stocks
- Real estate rental income
- Peer-to-peer lending
- REITs

Pros:

- Builds over time
- Tax-advantaged if done through IRAs, HSAs, etc.

Cons:

- Market risk
- Requires capital
- Some options (like real estate) can be more active than advertised

The goal here is to build a mix of income streams: some from your job, some from your brain (IP), and some from your money (investments).

Real-World Scenario: Diversified Engineer

Alex is a 42-year-old systems engineer with a wife and two kids. Here's his income breakdown:

- $135,000 salary
- $18,000 in dividends from ETFs
- $4,800 from an eBook on embedded systems
- $9,500 from licensing a sensor design to a robotics firm

His passive income streams now cover 25% of his expenses.

The Roadmap to Building Passive Income as an Engineer

1. Audit Your Skills: What do people already ask you for help with?
2. Choose a Model: IP licensing, digital products, or investments?
3. Start Small: One course. One patent. One portfolio.
4. Protect Your Work: Learn about copyright, trademarks, patents.
5. Promote Intelligently: Engineers struggle with marketing. Start with your own network.
6. Track Income Sources: Build a spreadsheet. Engineers love spreadsheets.
7. Reinvest Wisely: Use passive income to fund further assets.

Common Mistakes to Avoid

- Assuming passive = effortless. It's not. It's front-loaded.

- Doing everything solo. Get legal help for IP. Hire freelance help for editing, websites, etc.
- Underpricing your expertise. You've worked hard to gain your knowledge—don't give it away.
- Waiting for perfect. Engineers often delay launching because it's not "done enough." Start before you're ready.

Encouragement: You're More Capable Than You Think

If you've ever debugged a PLC, optimized a control system, or led a product rollout, you have the brain for this. Intellectual property and passive income are not outside your skillset—they're adjacent to it.

You already think in systems.

This chapter just helped you apply those systems to your money.

Keep Going

Building passive income is like engineering any new solution. Start with a prototype. Iterate. Launch. Improve.

Your future isn't built by wishful thinking. It's built by design.

And remember:

The smartest engineers don't guess with money—they model it, monitor it, and improve it over time.

Let your ideas work as hard as you do.

Let your money follow systems, not chaos.

And let your future be designed by intention, not default.

Part VI – Mid-Career Challenges: Scaling Up Financially

Part VI of *Financial Literacy for Engineers* tackles the unique financial challenges—and exciting opportunities—that arise in the mid-career stage, typically between ages 35 and 55. At this point, many engineers find themselves juggling higher salaries, growing families, mortgages, aging parents, and increasing pressure to "catch up" or scale their wealth. This section is designed to help you move from financial stability to financial growth with clarity, confidence, and control.

We explore how to navigate promotions, job transitions, and equity compensation without falling into lifestyle inflation. You'll learn how to evaluate risk with greater precision, invest more strategically, and think beyond saving—toward building. Topics include optimizing your 401(k) and taxable investments, managing stock options, buying real estate, protecting your income with insurance, and strategically using debt as a tool, not a trap.

Mid-career is also when many engineers begin to ask deeper questions: "Am I behind?" "Should I be doing more with my money?" "How do I align my financial life with my values?" This part addresses those concerns with systems thinking, decision frameworks, and real-world scenarios tailored to engineering minds. Whether you're looking to expand passive income, invest in a second home, start a side business, or take a sabbatical, Part VI will help you engineer a plan to scale up—without burning out.

This isn't just about having more money. It's about using what you've built so far to create leverage, stability, and freedom for the future.

Chapter 26: Preparing for Management or Leadership Roles

Let's say you've been an engineer for 8 to 15 years. You're known for delivering quality work, mentoring junior team members, and leading projects that consistently meet deadlines. Naturally, someone approaches you—maybe your boss, maybe a peer—and says, "You've got leadership potential. Have you ever thought about management?"

That moment can feel both validating and terrifying. You've spent years mastering your craft—debugging systems, writing clean code, optimizing workflows—and now you're being asked to trade some of that technical depth for meetings, strategy, budgets, performance reviews, and conflict resolution.

Welcome to the leadership track.

This chapter isn't about whether you should take that path. It's about preparing for it—mentally, financially, and strategically—so you don't just survive in leadership. You thrive in it. And you do it in a way that aligns with your values and long-term financial goals.

Why Engineers Often Struggle with the Transition

Let's get honest: many engineers feel conflicted about becoming managers.

On one hand, it's a sign of respect. A chance to shape the future of your team, your company, and maybe even your industry.

On the other hand, it means stepping away from the technical work that brought you joy, security, and identity. It means navigating people problems instead of solving mechanical or logical ones. It means leading without always having clear answers.

And financially? It means new questions:

- Will the pay increase be worth the extra stress?
- What happens to my stock options or bonuses?
- Do I need to change my insurance, benefits, or tax strategy?

Let's walk through it all.

The Mindset Shift: From Individual Contributor to Multiplier

As an engineer, you're trained to deliver output. As a manager, your job becomes multiplying the output of others. That's a big shift.

You're no longer judged solely on what you do, but on what your team accomplishes under your leadership.

That means:

- Delegating instead of doing
- Coaching instead of correcting
- Planning instead of reacting
- Listening instead of always solving

It also means learning new tools: budgeting, performance management, cross-functional coordination, stakeholder alignment. These aren't trivial. But they're learnable.

Action Step: Read "The Manager's Path" by Camille Fournier or "Radical Candor" by Kim Scott. These are excellent starting points.

Financial Implications of Moving into Management

Let's look at the money side.

Base Salary: In most industries, a move to management comes with a salary bump. This could be 10%–30%, depending on level and company.

Bonuses and Incentives: Many managerial roles include performance-based bonuses. These may depend on team outcomes, department KPIs, or company profitability.

Stock Options/Equity: If you're at a startup or public company, leadership roles may come with access to higher-tier equity grants. These can be incredibly valuable—but also come with vesting schedules, tax implications, and risk.

Benefits Changes: You may gain access to executive-level benefits, such as:

- Deferred compensation plans
- Enhanced health savings account (HSA) contributions
- Long-term incentive plans
- Leadership development stipends

Action Step: If offered a promotion, ask for a total compensation breakdown—not just salary. Understand the full picture.

Understanding the Tradeoffs

Here's the honest truth: leadership isn't for everyone. And that's okay.

Pros:

- Higher income ceiling
- Greater influence and decision-making power
- Broader career mobility
- Opportunity to shape culture and mentorship

Cons:

- More meetings, less building
- Emotional labor (conflict, performance issues)
- Accountability for others' work
- Risk of burnout without strong boundaries

Scenario: You're a 38-year-old project engineer offered a director role. It pays $30K more annually but comes with weekly travel and team accountability. You need to ask:

- Is this worth it for my lifestyle?
- Does this align with my long-term goals?
- Will this enable—or derail—my financial plan?

Preparing Financially for Leadership

If you're moving into a leadership role, here are the key financial areas to revisit:

1. Taxes

- Higher income may bump you into a new tax bracket.
- Equity compensation requires tax planning (especially ISOs vs. NSOs).
- Bonus income may be withheld at higher rates.

Action Step: Meet with a CPA to plan for the next tax year.

1. Retirement Contributions

- Maximize 401(k), especially if eligible for executive plans.
- Consider opening a backdoor Roth IRA.
- Use bonuses or RSUs to fund brokerage investments.

1. Insurance

- Review disability insurance. As your income rises, so does your need for income replacement.
- Check life insurance coverage. If others depend on you, make sure your policy reflects your new financial role.
- Explore umbrella insurance. If your leadership role includes legal risk, this is a simple safeguard.

1. Emergency Fund

- Your risk profile has changed. Maintain 6–12 months of expenses.
- This protects against burnout-based career shifts or unexpected transitions.

1. Estate Planning

- Update your will, beneficiary designations, and healthcare directives.
- If you now manage high-value assets or equity, this becomes even more important.

Action Step: Build a spreadsheet to simulate your new net income, savings capacity, and tax exposure. Update your financial plan with this data.

Leadership Skills Every Engineer Can Learn

You don't need an MBA to lead well. You do need:

- Emotional Intelligence: Understand your team's needs and motivations.
- Communication: Clear writing, assertive speaking, active listening.
- Time Management: Prioritize what only you can do. Delegate the rest.
- Strategic Thinking: Zoom out. See systems. Think in quarters, not days.
- Financial Acumen: Read P&Ls. Build budgets. Justify ROI.

Action Step: Take a course on leadership for technical professionals (many are offered by IEEE, ASME, or LinkedIn Learning).

Building a Personal Board of Advisors

Just like a startup has a board of directors, you need a personal advisory team:

- A mentor in leadership
- A peer outside your company

- A CPA or financial advisor
- A coach or therapist (yes, seriously)

These people help you think clearly, stay grounded, and course-correct.

Scenario: You're leading a team of 10 for the first time. You're unsure how to handle performance reviews. You call your mentor, who talks you through it calmly. That 30-minute call saves you weeks of stress and prevents a potential team issue.

Balancing Leadership with Life

Leadership often brings long hours, blurred boundaries, and mental load.

That's why it's critical to:

- Protect personal time like a product launch
- Build a morning routine that centers you
- Learn to say no without guilt
- Take real vacations (yes, even when the team is busy)

Your health, relationships, and peace of mind matter more than any promotion.

Remember: Leadership isn't just about guiding others. It's about leading yourself with integrity, discipline, and clarity.

What If You Want to Go Back?

Let's remove the stigma: not every engineer who tries management wants to stay in it. Some return to technical paths. Some shift to consulting, teaching, or freelancing.

That's okay.

You're not failing—you're iterating.

Having tried leadership only expands your value. You now understand:

- How business decisions get made
- What managers care about
- How to advocate for engineers from a place of experience

You're more valuable, not less.

Takeaways

- Leadership is a choice, not an obligation.
- Prepare mentally and financially before accepting a role.
- Learn to manage your energy, not just your time.
- Build your support system.
- Design your financial systems to support the added income—and added risk.

Encouragement

You're more capable than you think.

You've solved complex technical problems. You've shipped. You've debugged. You've documented when no one else wanted to.

Now, you're ready to lead.

And if you're not ready yet? That's okay, too. Bookmark this chapter. Come back when you are.

Because the smartest engineers don't guess with leadership. They model it, measure it, and grow into it.

Chapter 27: Managing Multiple Income Streams

Let's say you're an engineer with a good salary. That's one income stream. But maybe you also have a rental property. Maybe you've written a niche software package that's selling on Gumroad. Maybe you're consulting on the side, or you've invested in dividend-paying ETFs. Now you're managing income from different sources—and things are starting to get complicated.

Welcome to the world of multiple income streams.

This chapter is about helping you structure, manage, and optimize your multi-source income life. It's not just about making more money. It's about building a resilient system that's designed with purpose. It's about reducing single-source dependency. It's about financial antifragility—the ability to thrive even when your job, industry, or health gets disrupted.

Let's walk through it like engineers: systematically, thoughtfully, and with real-world action steps you can implement.

Why Engineers Are Uniquely Suited to Multiple Income Streams

Engineers are wired for systems thinking. You already:

- Automate workflows
- Debug and iterate
- Analyze cost-benefit tradeoffs
- Understand compounding and risk

Managing multiple income streams is just another system. And when done right, it can be one of the most powerful financial levers of your career.

Types of Income Streams

Let's categorize income streams into five main buckets:

1. Earned Income – W-2 or self-employed work
2. Investment Income – Dividends, interest, capital gains
3. Passive Income – Royalties, licensing, digital products
4. Business Income – Freelancing, consulting, side businesses
5. Real Estate Income – Rentals, REITs, flipping, syndications

Each one has its own tax treatment, volatility profile, and time requirements.

Understanding the Interplay

When you manage multiple streams, the real challenge isn't making the money. It's integrating them into a coherent strategy:

- How does your side business income affect your tax bracket?
- Should you form an LLC for consulting work?
- Can your rental losses offset W-2 income?
- What's the best way to reinvest passive income?

We'll tackle all of that.

Step One: Track Every Income Source

Before you optimize, you measure.

Build a simple spreadsheet:

- List each stream of income
- Track gross income, expenses, and net income monthly
- Note the time investment and seasonality

Columns might include:

- Source (e.g., W-2 job, dividends, Etsy shop)
- Type (earned, passive, investment, etc.)
- Frequency (monthly, quarterly, seasonal)
- Income (gross and net)
- Time spent (per week or month)

This shows you:

- Which streams are high-yield, low-effort
- Which require heavy lifting for small return
- Which could scale with more investment

Step Two: Understand the Tax Implications

Multiple income streams can move you into higher tax brackets or trigger unexpected tax events.

Key concepts to understand:

- Marginal vs. effective tax rate
- Self-employment tax (15.3%) for 1099 income
- Passive vs. active income rules
- Qualified dividends vs. ordinary income
- Tax-loss harvesting to offset capital gains

Scenario:

You make $120K in salary (W-2), $6K from freelancing, $8K in dividends, and $4K from selling a digital product.

- Your freelance income is subject to self-employment tax.
- Your dividends may be taxed at 15% depending on your bracket.
- Your digital product income may allow business deductions.

Action Step:

Hire a CPA who understands side hustles, royalties, and capital gains.

Don't wait until tax time. Build a proactive plan.

Step Three: Decide on Business Structure

If any of your side income involves freelancing, consulting, or selling products, consider forming a business entity.

Common options:

- Sole Proprietorship: Easy, default. But no liability protection.
- LLC: Offers protection and professionalism. Can choose tax treatment.
- S-Corp: May reduce self-employment tax if income is high enough.

Pros of an LLC:

- Write off business expenses (laptop, office, education)
- Legally separate income and assets
- Easier to open business bank accounts

Cons:

- Requires setup and annual maintenance
- May not be needed for very small income

Action Step:

If your non-W-2 income exceeds $10,000/year, consider forming an LLC and opening separate checking and credit accounts.

Step Four: Build Automation Into Your Financial System

Multiple income streams can mean chaotic money movement. You need automation.

Ideas:

- Set up automatic transfers to tax savings account (20–30% of side income)
- Route income into separate accounts (business vs. personal)
- Auto-contribute from all income sources to investments

- Use budgeting tools (YNAB, Monarch, Tiller) to aggregate your data

Goal: You shouldn't need to manually move money every time you get paid.

Action Step:

Create a "financial dashboard"—your own system that shows what's coming in, where it's going, and how it aligns with your goals.

Step Five: Prioritize Based on ROI and Alignment

Not all income is equal.

You want:

- High ROI: Net income per hour
- High alignment: Matches your values, strengths, and long-term goals
- Low drag: Doesn't drain your energy or compromise your day job

Example:

Let's compare two streams:

1. Airbnb rental earning $6,000/year, requires 10 hours/month
2. Freelance writing earning $4,000/year, requires 3 hours/month

Even though the Airbnb earns more, the writing has higher ROI per hour and less hassle.

Action Step:

Score your income streams. Rate them on profit, time, joy, and scalability.

Step Six: Diversify Without Overextending

It's tempting to chase five income streams at once. Don't.

Build depth before breadth.

- Nail one side hustle before starting another
- Grow one investment portfolio before experimenting
- Turn one product into a system before creating ten more

Remember: the goal isn't chaos—it's freedom.

Use your engineering mindset: Build, test, optimize, scale.

Real-World Examples

Scenario 1: Mid-Career Engineer With 3 Income Streams

Jenny is a 39-year-old civil engineer. Her income:

- $115K salary
- $12K from a rental condo
- $3,000 from a civil engineering course she created

She keeps 25% of rental income set aside for repairs and taxes. She reinvests her course income into a taxable brokerage account. She's slowly growing the course into a full-fledged business.

Scenario 2: Senior Engineer Approaching FIRE

Derrick is 50, working toward Financial Independence. His streams:

- $140K salary
- $24K in dividends
- $6K from occasional consulting
- $8K from a YouTube channel

His goal is to replace 80% of his salary with investment income by age 55. He tracks all cash flows in Excel and rebalances quarterly.

Step Seven: Reinvest With Intention

What do you do with the income?

Options:

- Reinvest in growth (ads, tools, skills)
- Save in tax-advantaged accounts (IRA, Solo 401(k))
- Pay down debt (mortgage, student loans)
- Build up your opportunity fund (for buying businesses, land, etc.)

The key is to give every dollar a job. You're not just earning—you're allocating.

Action Step:

Create an "Income Allocation Map" for each stream:

- What % goes to taxes?
- What % goes to savings?
- What % goes to reinvestment?
- What % goes to fun or lifestyle?

Step Eight: Prepare for Income Volatility

When you have one job, your income is stable. With five streams, things fluctuate.

That's why:

- You need a bigger emergency fund (6–12 months)
- You may want a line of credit or access to liquidity
- You need to budget based on your lowest 3-month average

Action Step:

Build your budget around conservative estimates. Use windfall months to bulk up reserves.

Avoid These Common Mistakes

- Overcommitting: Burnout kills productivity and profit.
- Undertracking: Flying blind leads to tax surprises.
- Mixing personal and business finances
- Reinventing the wheel: Use templates, hire help, systematize
- Not knowing your numbers: You can't improve what you don't measure

Encouragement

You're more capable than you think.

You already manage complex systems at work. Money is just another system. Income streams are just subsystems.

You don't need to master it all at once. You just need to build one smart stream at a time.

And as those streams converge, you gain something rare:

- Flexibility
- Optionality
- Leverage
- Peace of mind

You're not just working for money. You're letting your money—and your ideas—work for you.

Takeaways

- Start tracking every income source and its metrics
- Understand the tax and legal implications of each
- Automate your systems so you don't burn out
- Focus on alignment, not just dollars
- Reinvest with purpose, and build buffers against volatility

Remember

The smartest engineers don't guess with money.

They model it, monitor it, and improve it over time.

Let that be you.

Chapter 28: Advanced Retirement Planning Beyond 401(k)s

If you've made it to this chapter, odds are you're doing something right. You've been saving in your 401(k). Maybe you're even maxing it out. You've built a solid foundation, understand basic investment principles, and you're thinking long-term. But now you're asking a deeper question: What's next?

Because for engineers like you—those who earn well, think systematically, and want to optimize—not stopping at a 401(k) isn't just a choice. It's the next logical step.

This chapter is all about what comes after the basics. It's about understanding how to stack strategies, optimize tax outcomes, diversify retirement vehicles, and truly design a retirement system that fits your goals—not just your employer's default plan.

Whether you're 28 or 58, the tools and strategies in this chapter can help you build a retirement that isn't just sufficient—but strategic, flexible, and resilient.

Let's get into it.

Why 401(k)s Aren't Enough on Their Own

401(k)s are powerful. They offer tax-deferred growth, employer matching, and high contribution limits. But they have limitations:

- Limited investment choices
- Contribution limits ($23,000 for 2025 if under 50; $30,500 if 50+)

- Required minimum distributions (RMDs) after age 73
- Taxable withdrawals
- No access before age 59½ without penalties (except in special circumstances)

So while 401(k)s are a great tool, they're not the whole toolbox.

Let's look at what else belongs in your system.

Strategy #1: The Backdoor Roth IRA

Many engineers earn too much to contribute directly to a Roth IRA. In 2025, the income limit to contribute phases out completely at $161,000 (single) or $240,000 (married).

But there's a workaround: the Backdoor Roth.

Here's how it works:

1. Contribute to a traditional IRA (non-deductible)
2. Wait a few days for the contribution to post
3. Convert that contribution to a Roth IRA

Because you didn't take a deduction on the contribution, the conversion is generally tax-free (unless there are other pre-tax IRA funds involved).

Pros:

- Tax-free growth
- No RMDs
- Great for high earners

Cons:

- Pro-rata rule complicates things if you have other IRAs
- Extra paperwork at tax time (Form 8606)

Action Step:

If you're eligible and don't have other IRAs, consider opening a traditional and Roth IRA at the same custodian and setting up a backdoor Roth each year. Automate it.

Strategy #2: The Mega Backdoor Roth 401(k)

Some employers offer a 401(k) plan that allows after-tax contributions above the standard limit—up to a combined $69,000 in 2025 (employee + employer contributions + after-tax).

If allowed, you can:

- Contribute up to the limit after-tax
- Then roll over or convert that money to a Roth IRA or Roth 401(k)

It's like injecting your Roth savings with rocket fuel.

Example:

You max out your pre-tax 401(k): $23,000

Your employer matches $10,000

That leaves $36,000 of room for after-tax contributions

You contribute $30,000 after-tax, then roll it into your Roth IRA.

Pros:

- Massive Roth funding
- Compound growth tax-free
- Great for high-income engineers with excess cash flow

Cons:

- Not all employers allow it
- Requires proactive tracking and conversions

Action Step:

Ask your HR department if your plan allows after-tax contributions and in-plan Roth rollovers. If yes, consider dialing down taxable investing and routing extra cash flow here.

Strategy #3: Health Savings Account (HSA) as a Stealth Retirement Tool

If you have a high-deductible health plan (HDHP), you're eligible for an HSA. In 2025, contribution limits are $4,300 for individuals and $8,550 for families (+$1,000 if 55+).

Why is this such a powerful tool?

- Contributions are tax-deductible
- Growth is tax-free
- Withdrawals for qualified medical expenses are tax-free

Triple tax advantage.

And here's the kicker: After age 65, you can use HSA funds for anything (not just medical) without penalty. You'll just pay income tax—like a traditional IRA.

That makes it a powerful hybrid tool:

- Use it for retirement healthcare costs (likely to rise)
- Or as a backup retirement account

Action Step:

If you're healthy and can afford to pay medical expenses out of pocket, let your HSA grow. Don't touch it until retirement.

Strategy #4: Taxable Brokerage Accounts

Taxable accounts aren't retirement-specific—but they're crucial for flexibility.

They allow:

- No contribution limits
- No income phaseouts
- No early withdrawal penalties
- Capital gains treatment (often lower than ordinary income tax)

You can:

- Harvest losses to offset gains
- Use dividends as supplemental income
- Sell strategically in low-income years

They're especially useful in early retirement or FIRE scenarios—when you need money before 59½.

Action Step:

Open a joint taxable account or individual brokerage. Set up auto-transfers. Invest in low-cost index funds or ETFs. Be mindful of turnover and tax efficiency.

Strategy #5: Solo 401(k) or SEP IRA for Side Income

If you freelance, consult, or own a business, you can create your own retirement plan.

Solo 401(k):

- Contribute up to $69,000 total (employee + employer side)
- Roth option available
- More flexible and higher limits than SEP

SEP IRA:

- Simpler to set up
- Contribution is employer-only: up to 25% of net income, max $69,000

These plans allow you to shelter more income if you have multiple streams.

Real-World Scenario:

Jake is a full-time engineer making $160K and consults on the side, earning $30K. He maxes his work 401(k) and opens a Solo 401(k) for the side income, contributing another $6,000.

That's $29,000 saved for retirement—far beyond one 401(k).

Action Step:

If you have 1099 income, explore opening a Solo 401(k). You can open one by December 31, even if you don't fund it until tax time.

Strategy #6: Deferred Compensation Plans (NQDC)

If you're a senior-level engineer at a large company, you might be offered a non-qualified deferred compensation plan.

This lets you defer part of your salary or bonus into a plan where it grows tax-deferred.

Pros:

- Reduces taxable income now
- Defers taxes until retirement (possibly lower bracket)

Cons:

- Not protected like 401(k)s (subject to company's solvency)
- Less flexibility (must choose payout schedule in advance)

This tool is best for:

- Engineers in high tax brackets
- Stable employers
- Long-term thinkers

Action Step:

Work with a financial planner before enrolling. Understand your company's structure, default risk, and payout terms.

Strategy #7: Roth Conversions During Low-Income Years

Strategic Roth conversions allow you to move money from traditional to Roth accounts—paying taxes now, but avoiding them later.

This is useful when:

- You're in a lower-than-normal income year
- You retire early before RMDs and Social Security

Example:

You retire at 55. From 55–67, you convert $30K per year to a Roth IRA, staying in a 12% bracket. That reduces your future RMDs and creates tax-free income buckets.

Action Step:

Create a spreadsheet or use a planning software to model multi-year conversions. Aim to fill lower tax brackets efficiently.

Strategy #8: Real Estate for Retirement Income

While not a retirement account, real estate can play a big role in retirement:

- Cash flow from rentals
- Appreciation
- Tax advantages (depreciation, 1031 exchanges)

But it's not for everyone. Real estate requires capital, time, and risk management.

You can also invest passively through:

- Real Estate Investment Trusts (REITs)
- Syndications
- Private equity funds

Action Step:

If real estate appeals to you, start small. Learn the math. Run the numbers like an engineer.

Strategy #9: Pensions and Annuities

Rare, but worth mentioning.

Some government or legacy engineering jobs still offer pensions. If you're eligible:

- Know your vesting schedule
- Understand payout options (single vs. joint life)

You can also create your own pension using an annuity:

- Immediate annuities (buy now, get income for life)
- Deferred income annuities

Pros:

- Guaranteed income
- Longevity protection

Cons:

- Illiquid
- Often expensive
- Less flexible than self-managed assets

Action Step:

If security and simplicity matter more to you than growth, consider allocating a portion of your retirement to annuities.

Bringing It All Together: Building a Layered Retirement Plan

Here's what a multi-layered retirement system might look like:

- 401(k): Max out with employer match
- Backdoor Roth IRA: Build tax-free growth
- HSA: Stealth retirement account for medical
- Taxable brokerage: Flexibility and capital gains treatment
- Solo 401(k): Shelter side income
- Deferred compensation: Delay high-tax earnings
- Roth conversions: Shrink future RMDs
- Real estate: Diversify and cash flow
- Annuities or pensions: Guaranteed income layer

That's not overwhelming. That's a system.

Engineers build systems.

This is how you engineer retirement.

Encouragement

You're more capable than you think.

You already manage complexity at work—timelines, constraints, variables, deliverables. This is just another project. And you're the project manager.

Design a retirement system that works for your life, your income, and your goals.

Don't stop at the 401(k).

That's just the on-ramp.

Takeaways

- 401(k)s are great, but not enough
- Roth tools offer tax-free growth—use them
- HSAs can be stealth IRAs
- Taxable accounts = flexibility
- Business income opens new retirement plans
- Strategy trumps reaction. Plan ahead.

Reminder

The smartest engineers don't guess with money—they model it, monitor it, and improve it over time.

Build the system.

Stress test it.

Retire on purpose.

Chapter 29: Tax Optimization Strategies for High Earners

If you're reading this chapter, you're likely in a place many aspire to reach. You're earning well, maybe six figures or more. You've worked hard to get here. But now you're noticing something else—how much of your income disappears into taxes. And you're asking the right question:

"How do I keep more of what I earn—without cutting corners, without breaking the rules, and without feeling like I'm gambling with the IRS?"

This chapter is your blueprint for answering that question. It's for engineers who are strategic, methodical, and serious about optimizing every component of their financial system—especially the tax code.

Taxes are not just a necessary evil. They're a lever. And when you pull the right ones, you can reduce waste, increase efficiency, and boost your long-term wealth.

Let's break it all down—from deductions and credits to business structures, retirement vehicles, and advanced strategies.

Because the smartest engineers don't overpay taxes. They model them.

Understanding the Marginal Tax System

First, let's clarify how the U.S. tax system works. It's marginal. That means your income is taxed in layers, not all at once.

For 2025 (estimates):

- 10% on the first $11,600 (single)
- 12% up to $47,150

- 22% up to $100,525
- 24% up to $191,950
- 32% up to $243,725
- 35% up to $609,350
- 37% beyond that

Most high-earning engineers sit in the 24%–35% range. The key is to understand how to *control* which parts of your income hit which brackets.

Action Step:

Look at your last two years of tax returns. Note where your taxable income fell and what your effective tax rate was (total tax ÷ total income).

Tax Strategy #1: Max Out Tax-Advantaged Accounts

Before we get fancy, make sure you're using the basics:

- 401(k): Contribute up to $23,000 ($30,500 if over 50)
- HSA: Contribute $4,300 individual / $8,550 family (plus $1,000 catch-up if 55+)
- Backdoor Roth IRA: Use if your income exceeds Roth limits
- 529 Plan: For college savings; many states offer tax deductions

These are your low-hanging fruit. They reduce your taxable income and supercharge long-term growth.

Action Step:

Automate monthly transfers to all eligible tax-advantaged accounts. Revisit contribution amounts annually.

Tax Strategy #2: Understand the Power of Deductions vs. Credits

Deductions reduce your *taxable income.* Credits reduce your *tax liability.*

Examples:

- Deductions: 401(k) contributions, mortgage interest, charitable donations
- Credits: Child Tax Credit, Lifetime Learning Credit, Energy Efficiency Credit

Credits are more powerful dollar-for-dollar, but deductions are easier to control through smart spending.

Action Step:

Track deductible expenses throughout the year. Don't scramble in April—plan in January.

Tax Strategy #3: Use a Donor-Advised Fund (DAF) for Charitable Giving

If you give to charity, consider batching donations into a Donor-Advised Fund.

Example:

Instead of donating $5,000/year for 5 years, donate $25,000 this year. That lets you itemize this year, take the deduction, and distribute the money over time.

Pros:

- Get a big deduction in a high-income year
- Invest the funds tax-free until granted
- Still support causes you care about

Action Step:

Set up a DAF through a brokerage like Fidelity or Schwab. Use it to front-load charitable giving in high-income years.

Tax Strategy #4: Use Your HSA as a Retirement Account

An HSA is the only triple-tax-advantaged account:

- Contributions are tax-deductible
- Growth is tax-free
- Withdrawals are tax-free for medical expenses

If you pay medical expenses out of pocket and keep receipts, you can reimburse yourself tax-free in retirement—even decades later.

Action Step:

Contribute the maximum, invest the balance, and track receipts for future tax-free withdrawals.

Tax Strategy #5: Invest Tax-Efficiently in Brokerage Accounts

When investing outside of retirement accounts, tax efficiency matters.

Tips:

- Use index ETFs (low turnover = fewer capital gains)
- Harvest losses strategically to offset gains (tax-loss harvesting)
- Hold investments >1 year to benefit from long-term capital gains rates (0%, 15%, 20%)
- Avoid frequent trading that generates short-term gains (taxed as ordinary income)

Real-World Example:

Anna has $300K in a taxable brokerage. She sells a poorly performing fund for a $6,000 loss, which offsets gains from another sale, saving $1,200 in taxes.

Action Step:

Once per year, review your taxable account. Sell losers to offset gains. Reinvest wisely.

Tax Strategy #6: Manage Stock Options and RSUs Carefully

If you receive equity compensation (common in tech and engineering roles), tax planning is essential.

Restricted Stock Units (RSUs):

- Taxed as ordinary income when vested
- Capital gains apply to any increase after vesting

Incentive Stock Options (ISOs):

- No income tax at exercise
- But could trigger Alternative Minimum Tax (AMT)
- Favorable long-term capital gains if held 1 year from exercise and 2 years from grant

Non-Qualified Stock Options (NSOs):

- Taxed at exercise as ordinary income

Action Step:

Work with a CPA to time exercises and sales. Model AMT risk. Plan around vesting schedules.

Tax Strategy #7: Open a Solo 401(k) for Side Hustles

If you earn freelance income (consulting, design, tutoring, etc.), you can shelter more income using a Solo 401(k).

Contribution limits:

- Employee side: $23,000
- Employer side: Up to 25% of net business income (total $69,000 combined limit for 2025)

Action Step:

If you have side income, open a Solo 401(k) through a brokerage. Shelter as much income as possible.

Tax Strategy #8: Use Real Estate Strategically

Real estate offers powerful tax benefits:

- Depreciation shelters income
- 1031 exchanges defer capital gains
- Passive income taxed favorably
- You may deduct losses (if you qualify as a Real Estate Professional)

Even if you're not a landlord, investing in Real Estate Investment Trusts (REITs) offers income diversification.

Action Step:

If you own property, work with a CPA to maximize depreciation and structure deductions.

Tax Strategy #9: Defer Income or Accelerate Deductions

Timing matters.

In high-income years, consider:

- Deferring bonuses or freelance payments to next year
- Accelerating charitable giving or business expenses this year

This lets you smooth income and keep yourself in a lower bracket.

Scenario:

James expects a $20K bonus in December. He asks his employer to delay until January. That keeps him in the 24% bracket, saving $1,600.

Tax Strategy #10: Hire a Proactive CPA

This isn't just about filing your taxes. It's about *planning* for them.

A great CPA can:

- Model tax savings across multiple strategies
- Alert you to phaseouts and surtaxes
- Handle complex equity compensation
- Suggest quarterly estimated tax payments to avoid penalties

Action Step:

Interview 2–3 CPAs. Look for someone who *asks you questions,* not just fills in forms.

Advanced Topics for Engineers With Higher Complexity

- Qualified Small Business Stock (QSBS) exclusions
- Roth conversions in low-income years
- Asset location (put bonds in tax-advantaged, stocks in taxable)
- Tax deferral via installment sales or deferred comp
- Trusts for estate and income tax efficiency

Encouragement

You're more capable than you think.

Taxes feel overwhelming because the system is complex. But you've managed systems more complicated than this. You've built software, designed structures, optimized processes.

This is just another process. And you don't have to do it alone.

Takeaways

- Use every tax-advantaged account available
- Know your marginal bracket and model income
- Optimize timing of income and deductions
- Use real estate, equity comp, and business income intentionally
- Hire great professionals to help you navigate advanced strategies

The smartest engineers don't guess with money.

They model it.

They test it.

They improve it.

And over time, that's what builds real wealth.

Chapter 30: The Hidden Costs of Career Burnout

Let's talk about something most engineers won't bring up in a budget spreadsheet, tax planning session, or retirement forecast. It's not an investment portfolio issue. It's not a line item. It's not even tangible at first.

But it's real.

It's burnout.

And if you've been in the engineering field for more than a few years, you know exactly what I mean—even if you've never said the word out loud.

Burnout isn't just about being tired. It's not just about stress. It's not just having a rough month or a long week.

Burnout is when your output remains high, but your energy, focus, health, and joy quietly erode underneath.

And what often goes unnoticed—especially by engineers—is the financial cost of that erosion.

This chapter is about naming it, measuring it, and creating systems to protect yourself.

Because you can be great at managing money—and still lose wealth slowly, painfully, and invisibly to burnout.

Let's dig in.

What Burnout Really Looks Like for Engineers

It doesn't always show up as a breakdown.

For engineers, it's more often a slow drift:

- You dread checking your work email.
- You start missing deadlines or caring less about the ones you meet.
- You stop pursuing certifications, projects, or leadership roles.
- You find yourself snapping at coworkers—or going silent.
- You go home exhausted, even though you barely moved.

The problem isn't just emotional.

Burnout rewires your thinking. It shrinks your vision. It narrows your tolerance. It clouds your judgment.

And eventually—it shows up in your finances.

Let's look at how.

The Financial Cost of Burnout: A Layered Breakdown

Burnout is a wealth leak. It drains money not in one big splash—but in slow, compounding drips.

1. **Lost Raises and Promotions**
2. When you're disengaged, exhausted, or detached, you stop putting yourself in position to grow. You may:

- Miss out on annual raises
- Avoid leadership opportunities
- Get passed over for promotion

In a high-paying field like engineering, this stagnation compounds.

Scenario:

Mark, a talented mechanical engineer, starts tuning out. He's capable but unmotivated. Over 5 years, he watches peers jump from $110K to $150K while he stays flat. That $40K annual gap = $200K lost over five years, not including bonus and equity.

1. **Healthcare Costs**
2. Burnout impacts physical health.

- Chronic stress weakens the immune system
- Poor sleep raises the risk of heart disease
- Mental health struggles often lead to medication or therapy

And untreated burnout can escalate to medical leaves, surgeries, or emergency care.

It also affects those around you—spouses, children, colleagues.

1. **Productivity Decline**
2. When you're burned out, tasks take longer.

- You lose your edge.
- You make more mistakes.
- You spend more time fixing problems you used to prevent.

Even if you're salaried, this affects your long-term output, reputation, and value.

1. **Early Exit or Career Change**
2. Burned-out engineers often fantasize about quitting—sometimes without a plan.

- Some exit the field prematurely.
- Others downshift into lower-paying jobs just to escape the pressure.
- Many never reenter their peak earning years.

This is a hidden six-figure mistake.

Scenario:

Jessica earns $180K as a senior software engineer. She burns out, takes a sabbatical, and reenters at $110K in a support role. That $70K gap over 10 years = $700,000 lost.

1. **Impaired Decision-Making**

2. Burnout leads to:

- Delayed decisions
- Emotional spending
- Short-term thinking
- Missed investment opportunities

You might:

- Avoid rebalancing your 401(k)
- Stay in a toxic job too long
- Pull out of the market during a downturn

These choices have long-term ripple effects.

1. **Strained Relationships**
2. Burnout often leaks into personal life:

- Arguments about work or money
- Lack of presence with family
- Disconnection from support systems

Divorce, missed memories, lost friendships—all carry emotional and financial cost.

What Causes Engineer Burnout?

You already know the answers.

- Too many projects, not enough time
- Ambiguous expectations
- Lack of recognition
- Poor leadership
- Constant change
- Technical debt and impossible timelines

But there are financial triggers, too:

- Living paycheck to paycheck despite six-figure income
- Golden handcuffs (you can't leave a job because of equity or benefits)
- Career stagnation despite financial "success"
- Constant pressure to level up, with no reprieve

And don't forget the identity piece:

Many engineers link their *worth* to their *work*. When work becomes toxic, it doesn't just threaten your job—it threatens your sense of self.

Strategies to Prevent or Recover from Burnout—Financially and Personally

Let's build a system.

Not just for managing burnout—but for preventing it.

1. **Create a Career Buffer Fund**
2. Burnout is harder to manage when you feel trapped.

A career buffer fund = 6–12 months of living expenses set aside so you can:

- Take a break
- Change jobs
- Start a business
- Pursue something with less pressure

Action Step:

Open a high-yield savings account labeled "Career Buffer." Build it like a project.

1. **Reevaluate Your Financial Goals**
2. Sometimes, burnout stems from chasing someone else's version of success.

Questions to ask:

- Do I really need to retire by 45?
- Is the second home actually part of my vision?
- Am I working for a lifestyle I don't even enjoy?

Financial clarity can ease pressure. You may not need to push so hard.

1. **Redesign Your Workload with Margin**
2. You can engineer your calendar like you'd engineer a product.

- Block work sprints and recovery time
- Protect deep work windows
- Build non-negotiable off-grid time

Work expands to fill the time you allow. Shrink the container.

1. **Invest in Mental Health as a Line Item**
2. Therapy, coaching, or support groups aren't luxuries. They're maintenance.

Budget for them.

- $150/month on therapy may save you $15,000 in bad decisions
- Coaching may unlock the clarity to negotiate a raise or pivot careers

Action Step:
Add "Mental Maintenance" to your budget. Fund it monthly.

1. **Outsource or Simplify Where You Can**
2. Burnout doesn't always come from work.

- Household tasks

- Financial decisions
- Family obligations

Consider:

- Hiring a house cleaner
- Using a robo-advisor
- Automating meal planning or grocery delivery

Outsource the drain so you can preserve energy for the priorities.

1. **Know the Signs—And Listen Early**

- You dread Mondays for months in a row
- You stop caring about the quality of your work
- You're constantly tired, even after sleep
- You fantasize about disappearing, not retiring

Don't wait until you break. Intervene early.

1. **Build a Peer Network for Venting and Validation**
2. You're not the only one burned out.
3. But engineers often isolate.

- Find safe spaces: Slack groups, alumni forums, mastermind circles
- Share what you're navigating
- Learn how others handle the same stress

Support helps.

1. **Have a "Quit Plan" on Paper**
2. Even if you don't intend to quit, having a plan reduces anxiety.

- What's your runway?
- What jobs could you pivot to?
- What skills would you need?

The knowledge that you *could* leave makes staying feel less suffocating.

Real-World Scenarios

Scenario 1: The High Earner With No Time

David makes $220K as a systems engineer. He hasn't taken a real vacation in 3 years. His stress is affecting his marriage and sleep.

He hires a financial planner, figures out he can downshift to a $160K job and still hit his goals. He quits, joins a smaller firm, and rebuilds margin.

Scenario 2: The Burned-Out Early Retiree

Tina is 44. She hit her FIRE number. But instead of joy, she feels lost. She realizes she burned out to escape work, not build a life.

She starts working part-time in consulting, joins a coaching circle, and slowly rebuilds purpose—without pressure.

Encouragement

You're more capable than you think.

Burnout isn't a personal failure. It's a system overload.

And you already know how to rebuild systems.

You just have to treat your energy like your codebase, your project scope, or your product lifecycle.

Design for uptime.

Design for resilience.

Design for sustainability.

Takeaways

- Burnout has hidden financial costs: missed raises, poor decisions, early exits
- Prevention is cheaper than repair—build margin before crisis
- Your money should serve your life, not just your status
- Engineer your career like a system: with breaks, buffers, and feedback loops

The smartest engineers don't just build wealth.

They build lives that don't burn them out in the process.

Part VII – Managing Risk Like an Engineer

Part VII of *Financial Literacy for Engineers* focuses on one of the most overlooked yet essential pillars of long-term wealth: risk management. Engineers are trained to anticipate failure points, build redundancies, and stress-test systems before they fail. This section applies that same mindset to your financial life—so you don't just build wealth, you protect it.

From insurance planning to legal safeguards, from emergency funds to asset protection, this part helps you think through risks logically, not emotionally. You'll learn how to evaluate disability, life, liability, and long-term care insurance—not as a sales pitch, but as part of a defensive strategy. You'll explore how to mitigate financial shocks from career interruptions, health issues, lawsuits, and market volatility.

Real-world examples ground the concepts in relatable scenarios, whether you're a 29-year-old engineer with a growing net worth or a 55-year-old with more to lose than ever before. You'll design systems to handle risk the same way you would approach failure modes in a product: with foresight, structure, and control.

This part isn't about fear—it's about building resilience. It's about protecting your ability to earn, your assets, your family, and your peace of mind. Because in the end, risk isn't something to avoid. It's something to understand, quantify, and manage—like an engineer.

Chapter 31: Insurance 101 – What You Need, What You Don't

Let's start with a simple truth most people avoid: Insurance isn't exciting.

It's not fun to shop for. It's not thrilling to read about. No one dreams of calling their insurance agent.

But here's the other truth: Insurance is one of the most important tools in your financial system. Especially if you're an engineer earning well, raising a family, managing assets, or planning for retirement.

Because if something goes wrong—a car accident, a disability, a fire, a lawsuit, a major illness—insurance isn't just a document. It's the firewall that keeps your life from falling apart.

In this chapter, we'll walk through the core types of insurance you need to understand, which ones are essential, which ones are optional, and which ones are overpriced distractions. No scare tactics. No upselling. Just logic, structure, and clarity.

Let's start with the big question: Why does insurance matter to your financial life?

Insurance = Risk Transfer

As an engineer, you manage systems. You think in probabilities and consequences. You've probably heard this before:

Risk = Probability x Impact

In other words:

- Some things are unlikely but devastating
- Others are likely but manageable

Insurance isn't about preventing bad things from happening. It's about minimizing the *financial* damage when they do.

So your job is to:

1. Identify risks
2. Measure the financial impact
3. Decide whether to self-insure (absorb it) or transfer the risk (buy insurance)

With that framework in mind, let's go category by category.

Health Insurance: Non-Negotiable

This is the one insurance you absolutely cannot afford to go without.

Even a simple ER visit or surgery can cost tens of thousands. A cancer diagnosis or serious illness can bankrupt a six-figure earner in a year.

If you're employed:

- Choose between high-deductible and traditional PPO/HMO plans
- Consider your total cost: premium + deductible + coinsurance + out-of-pocket max

High-deductible health plans (HDHPs) paired with Health Savings Accounts (HSAs) can be very efficient for healthy individuals and families.

If you're self-employed:

- Shop on the ACA marketplace or through a professional organization
- Deduct premiums as a business expense

What to skip:

- Accident-only or hospital indemnity plans unless you truly lack other options

Action Step:

Run a "worst-case scenario" spreadsheet each year: How much would you pay out of pocket if you had a major medical event? Is your plan protecting you?

Disability Insurance: Often Overlooked, Critically Important

If you're a high-earning engineer, your biggest asset isn't your 401(k). It's your future income.

Disability insurance protects that income if you can't work due to injury or illness.

There are two types:

- Short-term disability (usually up to 3-6 months)
- Long-term disability (kicks in after short-term ends and can last for years)

You need long-term disability. Period.

Key things to check:

- Definition of disability (own occupation vs. any occupation)
- Benefit period (to age 65 is ideal)
- Elimination period (how long you wait before benefits start)

If you're employed, your company may offer basic group disability coverage. It's usually limited (e.g., 60% of salary) and may be taxable.

Consider buying supplemental private coverage, especially if:

- You earn over $150K
- You rely on bonuses or equity that wouldn't be covered

What to skip:

- Overpaying for riders you don't need (e.g., cost-of-living increases in your 20s)

Action Step:

Ask HR for a copy of your disability policy. If it's insufficient, get a quote from an independent broker.

Life Insurance: Depends on Who Depends on You

You only need life insurance if someone depends on your income to survive.

That includes:

- Spouse or partner who would struggle without your income
- Children who rely on your support
- Business partners with whom you share financial obligations

If no one relies on you, you don't need life insurance.

Term life insurance is almost always the right answer:

- Simple
- Affordable
- Covers you for a set number of years (10, 20, or 30)

Avoid permanent life insurance (whole life, universal life) unless:

- You've maxed out every other tax-advantaged account
- You need lifelong coverage for estate planning
- You understand the structure and cost thoroughly

How much do you need?

- Enough to replace your income for 10–20 years
- Enough to pay off your mortgage, cover college costs, or meet other big goals

What to skip:

- Life insurance as an "investment" unless you've done the math
- Policies offered through work as your only coverage (they usually don't go with you when you leave)

Action Step:

Use an online calculator (or spreadsheet) to estimate how much your dependents would need if you were gone tomorrow. Then get quotes on a 20- or 30-year term policy.

Auto Insurance: More Than Just Legal Compliance

Every state requires auto insurance. But not every policy is created equal.

Focus on:

- Liability coverage (bodily injury and property damage)
- Uninsured/underinsured motorist coverage
- Collision and comprehensive (if your car has value)

Rule of thumb: Don't skimp on liability. One bad accident can wipe out your savings.

What to skip:

- Paying extra for roadside assistance or rental car unless you actually use it

Action Step:

Compare your current policy to at least 2 others. Shop every 1–2 years. Increasing your deductible can save on premiums.

Homeowners or Renters Insurance: Protect Your Property

If you own a home:

- Homeowners insurance covers damage to your structure and personal belongings

- It also includes liability protection

Make sure you're covered for:

- Replacement cost (not just cash value)
- Water damage (not always included)
- Earthquake or flood (often separate policies)

If you rent:

- Renters insurance is cheap and protects your stuff—and your liability

Action Step:

Do a home inventory (photos + spreadsheet). Keep it in the cloud. It'll be priceless in a claim.

Umbrella Insurance: The Hidden Hero of Risk Management

Umbrella insurance provides extra liability coverage on top of your auto and home policies.

It's designed to protect your assets if you're sued.

For example:

- You cause a major car accident
- Someone sues you after a dog bite, injury on your property, or false accusation

If you have over $300,000 in assets (including equity, investments, or income), umbrella insurance is smart.

Coverage often starts at $1 million and costs $150–300/year.

Action Step:

Call your insurance provider and ask for an umbrella policy quote. You may need to increase liability limits on your auto and home first.

Other Insurance Types: Evaluate, Don't Ignore

There are dozens of niche insurance products out there. Here's a breakdown:

Long-Term Care Insurance:

- Consider in your 50s if you have assets to protect
- Covers nursing home or in-home care later in life

Pet Insurance:

- Worth it for expensive breeds or if you'd go into debt for surgery

Travel Insurance:

- Valuable for international trips, medical evacuation, or high-cost itineraries

Identity Theft Insurance:

- Some credit cards or employers offer it for free

Critical Illness Insurance:

- Pays a lump sum if diagnosed with major illness; good for those with minimal savings

Gadget or Appliance Insurance:

- Usually a waste. Save the premium and self-insure.

What to Remember

Insurance isn't about maximizing returns. It's about minimizing regret.
You don't win by avoiding all insurance.
You win by buying the right amount of the right kind—at the right time.
Think like an engineer:

- What are the failure modes of your life?
- What are the consequences?
- How do you create a safety net that makes the rest of your system more stable?

Encouragement

You're more capable than you think.

It's easy to ignore insurance because it's boring or confusing. But you've debugged harder code. You've optimized more complex systems.

You can structure this, too.

Takeaways

- Health insurance is essential—optimize for total cost, not just premiums
- Disability insurance is a must for high earners—protect your income
- Term life insurance is usually sufficient—skip the complexity unless you've outgrown the basics
- Auto, home, and umbrella insurance protect against major liability
- Other policies should be evaluated based on risk exposure and personal priorities

Final Reminder

Insurance isn't just a bill. It's a system of backups, buffers, and contingencies.

The smartest engineers don't guess with risk.

They design around it.

They model it.

They protect the system they've worked hard to build.

You can, too.

Chapter 32: Life Insurance – Term vs. Whole Life Explained Simply

Let's talk about one of the most confusing—and most aggressively marketed—financial products you'll encounter as an engineer: life insurance.

You've probably heard strong opinions on both sides:

"Just buy term and invest the rest."

"Whole life is a scam."

"You're missing out on tax-free growth."

"Only rich people need permanent life insurance."

So which is it?

This chapter is here to cut through the noise and help you understand life insurance in a way that makes logical, financial sense.

Not from a salesperson.

Not from a YouTube rant.

From the perspective of someone like you—an engineer who thinks in systems, risk mitigation, and long-term outcomes.

We'll look at what life insurance is for, how it works, and the real differences between term and whole life. Then we'll explore use cases, pros and cons, and how to decide what *you* actually need.

Start With Purpose: What Is Life Insurance *For*?

Life insurance is a financial tool with one main purpose:

To provide a lump sum of money to someone if you die unexpectedly and your income or role was critical to their financial security.

That's it.

It's not an investment first.

It's not a savings plan first.

It's a form of protection.

So the first question isn't: "Which kind should I buy?"

The first question is: "Does anyone rely on me financially, and what would they need if I were gone tomorrow?"

If no one depends on you, and you have no major debts that could burden your family—congratulations. You may not need life insurance at all right now.

But if someone *does* depend on you, keep reading.

Term Life Insurance – Simple, Efficient, and Affordable

Term life insurance covers you for a fixed period of time—typically 10, 20, or 30 years. If you die during that term, your beneficiary gets the death benefit (say, $500,000 or $1 million).

If you outlive the term, the policy expires. There's no payout. You're not refunded your premiums.

Term is like renting insurance: You pay to be covered for a set period, and then it ends.

Pros:

- Very affordable
- High coverage for low cost
- Simple and easy to understand
- Ideal for temporary needs (e.g., until your kids are grown or mortgage is paid)

Cons:

- No cash value or investment component
- You get nothing if you outlive the term
- Premiums can rise sharply if you try to renew later in life

Term is usually the best choice for:

- Young families
- Primary earners with dependents
- People looking to replace income, pay off a mortgage, or fund education if they die prematurely

Real-World Example:

David, a 35-year-old software engineer with a wife and two young kids, buys a $1 million 20-year term policy for $45/month. If he dies in the next 20 years, his family has a financial safety net. After 20 years, his kids are out of college, the mortgage is paid, and the coverage ends. No payout—but no longer needed.

Whole Life Insurance – Permanent Coverage With Cash Value

Whole life insurance is a form of permanent insurance. It covers you for your entire life—as long as you keep paying premiums. It also builds cash value, which grows over time and can be borrowed against or withdrawn.

Think of it as two things bundled together:

1. A life insurance policy
2. A forced savings account

You pay higher premiums than term life, but part of that money is set aside and grows tax-deferred.

Pros:

- Permanent coverage (your beneficiaries will be paid whenever you die)
- Builds cash value you can borrow from
- Premiums remain level
- Can be used for estate planning or wealth transfer

Cons:

- Expensive (10–20x more than term for the same death benefit)
- Cash value grows slowly early on
- Fees and commissions are high
- Returns are usually lower than investing elsewhere

Whole life *can* make sense if:

- You've maxed out all other retirement and tax-advantaged options
- You have a lifelong dependent (e.g., special-needs child)
- You're doing estate planning and want to leave a guaranteed legacy
- You have a high net worth and want another place for tax-deferred growth

Real-World Example:

Sara, a 50-year-old engineer with a disabled adult child, buys a $250,000 whole life policy for $500/month. The death benefit is guaranteed, and she likes knowing the cash value is growing tax-deferred. She's already maxed out her 401(k), Roth IRA, and HSA.

Term vs. Whole Life – Side-by-Side Comparison

Feature Term Life Whole Life

Duration

Temporary (10–30 years)

Lifetime

Cost

Low

High

Cash Value

None

Yes

Premiums

Level during term

Level for life

Investment

No

Yes (built-in)

Goal

Replace income if you die young

Legacy, estate planning, forced savings

Common Engineer Questions

"Should I get both?"

Possibly. Some high earners use term life for income protection and small whole life policies for legacy or diversification purposes.

"Can I invest the difference instead of buying whole life?"

Yes, and in most cases, you should. If you can get $1M term for $50/month, and whole life for $500/month, that's $450/month you could invest elsewhere.

"What if I want insurance to cover estate taxes or leave a legacy?"

That's where permanent insurance can shine—especially if structured correctly and held in a trust.

"What about variable or universal life policies?"

These are hybrids that mix insurance with more complex investment components. They require careful modeling and aren't usually necessary unless you're in advanced planning territory.

Action Steps

1. **Assess your need**

- Who relies on your income?
- What would they need to be okay if you were gone?

1. **Get quotes**

- Use online comparison tools to price 20- or 30-year term policies
- Compare to a whole life quote if you're curious—but look at the internal rate of return, not just the sales pitch

1. **Choose a reputable insurer**

- Stick with companies rated A or better by AM Best

1. **Review every few years**

- As life changes (marriage, kids, home, job), your needs may change

1. **Avoid tying life insurance to your employer**

- Group policies can be fine as a bonus, but aren't portable and often have low limits

What Not to Do

- Don't buy more coverage than you need "just in case"
- Don't skip insurance just because you're healthy and young
- Don't buy permanent life insurance until you've maxed out 401(k)s, Roth IRAs, and HSAs
- Don't mix insurance and investing without fully understanding the trade-offs

Encouragement

You're more capable than you think.

Life insurance can feel overwhelming. But it's not that different from other systems you've designed or optimized. Define the goal. Model the inputs. Choose the cleanest solution.

For most engineers, term life is the right tool. It's cost-effective, straightforward, and protective.

If you reach a point where your financial life is layered, complex, and tax-sensitive—then permanent life insurance may become a valuable tool in your portfolio. But it should be a second-tier decision, not a first-step move.

Takeaways

- Life insurance is for income replacement—not investment returns
- Term life is usually the best starting point for most engineers
- Whole life has a role, but only in specific advanced scenarios
- Your financial plan should determine your insurance—not the other way around

The smartest engineers don't overinsure or underinsure.

They right-size.

They simplify.

They protect the system.

Chapter 33: Disability Insurance for Engineers – Why It's Critical

Let's get right to it: If you're an engineer, your ability to think clearly, solve problems, write code, manage teams, draw designs, or build systems *is* your most valuable asset.

Not your 401(k).

Not your stock options.

Not even your home.

It's your *income-generating ability.*

That ability could be worth millions over the course of your career. And yet, most engineers have no protection in place if it disappears.

That's where disability insurance comes in.

This chapter will walk you through what disability insurance is, why it's often misunderstood, and how to decide what kind you actually need. We'll go beyond theory and explore real numbers, common scenarios, and engineer-specific examples.

Because the smartest engineers don't just build wealth.

They protect the system.

Let's start with a question:

What would happen to your finances if you couldn't work for the next six months? Or six years? Or ever again?

What Is Disability Insurance?

Disability insurance is income protection.

If you become too sick or injured to work, it replaces a portion of your income—so your bills still get paid, your savings aren't drained, and your long-term goals stay intact.

It doesn't matter how much you've saved. If you're in your 30s, 40s, or 50s and you lose your income permanently, your financial plan crumbles.

Disability insurance exists to prevent that collapse.

There are two main types:

1. **Short-Term Disability** – Covers you for a few weeks or months, often provided by employers. It might pay benefits for 3 to 6 months.
2. **Long-Term Disability** – Kicks in after a waiting period (often 90 or 180 days) and can pay benefits for years, or until retirement.

As a high-earning engineer, **long-term disability is the one you need to focus on.**

Why Engineers Are Particularly Vulnerable

Let's say you're a 34-year-old civil engineer making $130,000 a year. You plan to work another 30 years.

That's nearly $4 million in future income, assuming zero raises or promotions.

Now imagine a skiing accident, a chronic illness, or a condition like multiple sclerosis, long COVID, or cancer.

Even if you're healthy today, the stats are sobering:

- 1 in 4 people in their 20s will experience a disabling event before age 67
- The average long-term disability claim lasts over 34 months
- Most disabilities are caused by illness, not injury

And here's the kicker: Workman's comp only covers *on-the-job* injuries. Social Security Disability is notoriously hard to qualify for and pays very little.

So unless your employer has robust long-term disability coverage—and many don't—you're on your own.

What Disability Insurance Covers (And What It Doesn't)

Disability insurance doesn't cover medical bills—that's what health insurance is for.

Instead, it pays you a portion of your *lost income* if you can't work due to illness or injury.

Policies typically cover 60%–70% of your pre-disability income. But there are caveats:

- Group policies may cap your benefit (e.g., $5,000/month), which may not fully cover high earners
- Benefits from employer-paid plans are usually *taxable*
- Benefits from self-paid plans are usually *tax-free*

A good policy will pay until:

- You return to work
- You reach retirement age (usually 65 or 67)
- Or you die

But not all policies are created equal. Let's look at key features.

Key Features of Long-Term Disability Policies

1. **Own-Occupation vs. Any-Occupation**
2. This is the *most critical feature* for engineers.

- **Own-Occupation**: You're considered disabled if you can't perform your specific job (e.g., software architect), even if you could do something else (e.g., tech support).
- **Any-Occupation**: You're only considered disabled if you can't perform *any* job for which you're reasonably qualified.

Always opt for **own-occupation**. It's more expensive, but it protects your actual income level and training.

1. **Benefit Amount**

- Usually replaces 60%–70% of gross income
- Private policies may allow you to supplement group coverage
- You can't insure 100% of your income—insurers want you to have an incentive to return to work

1. **Benefit Period**

- 2 years, 5 years, or to age 65/67
- Aim for the longest period you can afford—this is what protects retirement savings

1. **Elimination Period (Waiting Period)**

- How long you wait before benefits begin
- Usually 90 or 180 days
- The longer the elimination period, the lower the premium

1. **Residual or Partial Disability Rider**

- Allows partial payments if you can return to work part-time or at reduced capacity

1. **Non-Cancelable and Guaranteed Renewable**

- Means your policy can't be canceled or changed as long as you pay premiums

1. **Future Increase Option**

- Lets you increase coverage later without medical underwriting
- Important for younger engineers who expect rising income

Pros and Cons of Private Disability Insurance

Pros:

- Tax-free income if you pay premiums yourself
- Customizable to your needs
- Goes with you if you change jobs
- Can supplement employer coverage

Cons:

- Premiums can be expensive (1%–3% of income)
- Requires medical underwriting
- May exclude pre-existing conditions

How to Evaluate Employer-Provided Coverage

Ask HR for your Summary Plan Description (SPD) and look for:

- Benefit percentage and maximum payout
- Definition of disability (own vs. any occupation)
- Whether bonuses or commissions are included
- Elimination period and benefit period
- Portability (can you keep it if you leave the job?)

If your employer plan is capped, taxable, or vague—you need a supplemental policy.

Real-World Engineer Scenarios

Scenario 1: Matt, 29, Aerospace Engineer

Matt earns $95K and has $2,000/month of coverage through work. He breaks his leg skiing and can't stand for long periods—he's out for 8 months. The policy has a 90-day waiting period, then pays $2,000/month.

That's only $12,000 in total—not nearly enough. He uses credit cards to cover the rest.

Lesson: Employer policies often fall short. Do the math.

Scenario 2: Neha, 42, Software Developer

Neha earns $180K, is single, and maxes out her 401(k). She gets diagnosed with a neurological disorder and can't code for more than 30 minutes at a time. Her private own-occupation policy replaces $8,500/month, tax-free. Her financial plan stays intact.

Lesson: For high earners, private coverage can be the difference between surviving and thriving.

Scenario 3: James, 38, Civil Engineer with Side Hustles

James makes $120K at his main job and $25K from part-time consulting. His employer plan doesn't cover side income. He buys a private policy that covers both streams.

Lesson: If you earn multiple incomes, structure coverage accordingly.

How Much Coverage Should You Buy?

Enough to:

- Pay your monthly expenses
- Continue retirement contributions
- Avoid tapping into savings or going into debt

If your budget is tight, buy a base policy now and increase later. Something is better than nothing.

Action Steps

1. **Inventory your income sources and fixed expenses**

- What does it take to maintain your life if income stopped?

1. **Request your employer's long-term disability plan details**

- Check for benefit % and caps
- Confirm own-occupation language

1. **Get quotes from at least two independent brokers**

- Ask for policies with own-occupation, residual, and future increase riders

1. **Consider bundling with life or umbrella insurance to save**
2. **Reevaluate every few years as your income changes**

Common Objections and Misconceptions

"I'm healthy—why would I need this?"

That's *why* you can get good rates now. You don't buy it for today—you buy it for what could happen tomorrow.

"It's too expensive."

Would you insure a $1 million house and not a $3 million career? You can adjust the benefit or elimination period to lower the premium.

"Won't Social Security take care of me?"

Social Security Disability pays very little, is hard to qualify for, and can take years to approve.

"I'll just use savings."

Even a $200,000 emergency fund can evaporate in 2 years without income. Most people don't have anywhere near that.

Encouragement

You're more capable than you think.

Disability insurance isn't glamorous. It's not exciting. But it's foundational.

It's the contingency plan that lets you sleep at night.

It's the system that holds the rest of your financial architecture together when life punches you in the face.

And you already know how to design systems with fail-safes.

Takeaways

- Your income is your greatest asset—protect it
- Long-term disability is essential for engineers
- Own-occupation coverage is non-negotiable
- Employer policies are often insufficient

- A well-structured private policy can protect your goals, your family, and your peace of mind

The smartest engineers don't ignore rare-but-ruinous risks.

They design around them.

They build in resilience.

Chapter 34: Umbrella Insurance – An Engineer's Extra Layer of Protection

You've built a career, a reputation, and likely a solid financial foundation.

You've got the basics covered:

- Health insurance? Check.
- Auto and homeowners insurance? Check.
- Disability and term life? Covered.

But here's the question most engineers don't think to ask:

What happens if all of that still isn't enough?

Let's say you get into a car accident, and the other driver sues you for $1.5 million.

Your auto policy only covers $300,000 in liability. Who's covering the other $1.2 million?

If you don't have umbrella insurance, the answer is: *you.*

Your savings.

Your investments.

Your future income (in some states).

This chapter is about protecting the financial system you've worked so hard to build.

Umbrella insurance isn't flashy. It doesn't get much attention in financial media.

But it's one of the most efficient risk management tools available—especially for high-earning, high-net-worth professionals like engineers.

Let's walk through what umbrella insurance is, how it works, and why it might be the missing piece in your financial firewall.

What Is Umbrella Insurance?

Umbrella insurance is a type of personal liability insurance.

It sits *on top* of your existing auto and homeowners (or renters) insurance.

When those policies reach their payout limit, the umbrella policy kicks in to cover the rest.

Think of it like this:

- Your auto policy might cover \$250,000 per person or \$500,000 per accident
- Your umbrella policy adds \$1 million or more in additional protection *after* those limits are exhausted

It doesn't just cover car accidents—it can also apply to:

- Injuries on your property
- Lawsuits for slander, libel, or defamation
- Dog bites
- Rental property incidents
- Volunteer or board service liability

If someone sues you—and the damages exceed your base coverage—the umbrella policy pays before your personal assets are on the line.

Why Engineers Should Care

You're a target. Not because of who you are, but because of what you've built.

If you:

- Earn a high income
- Own a home or multiple properties

- Have investments, savings, or equity
- Drive regularly or have teenage drivers
- Serve on a board or coach youth sports

Then your liability exposure is higher than average.

In a lawsuit, attorneys often look at what's *available.* They'll pursue the largest judgment they think they can collect.

Umbrella insurance creates a buffer—a legal and financial wall between a lawsuit and your future.

How Much Does It Cost?

Here's the best part: It's cheap.

A $1 million umbrella policy usually costs:

- $150–$300 per year
- Maybe $75–$100 per additional million in coverage

That's incredible leverage.

For less than $1/day, you could be protecting your entire net worth.

Compare that to the cost of not having it:

- A $1 million lawsuit = financial devastation
- Even if you win, legal fees alone can exceed $100,000

Umbrella insurance typically covers legal defense costs as well—even if you're not found liable.

What Umbrella Insurance Does *Not* Cover

Like every insurance product, umbrella policies have exclusions.

They don't cover:

- Your own injuries or damage to your property
- Intentional or criminal acts
- Business activities (unless endorsed)
- Contract disputes

- Professional malpractice (use a separate policy)

If you own a business or do freelance engineering work, make sure you have professional liability or errors & omissions coverage separately.

How It Works in a Claim Scenario

Let's say you're driving to a client site and accidentally run a red light. You collide with a minivan carrying a family of four. One passenger suffers permanent injury.

The family sues. The jury awards $1.8 million in damages.

Your auto policy pays out its maximum liability limit: $500,000.

Your umbrella policy kicks in and pays the remaining $1.3 million.

Without the umbrella coverage, you'd be forced to:

- Liquidate savings or retirement accounts
- Refinance or sell your home
- Face wage garnishment in some states

That's not fear-mongering—it's how liability law works.

Umbrella Coverage Requirements

To get an umbrella policy, insurers usually require:

- Auto liability limits of at least $250,000/$500,000
- Homeowners liability limits of at least $300,000

You may need to increase your base policies to qualify, which can raise those premiums slightly.

But it's worth it.

Because if you're carrying only $100,000 in auto liability coverage, you're wildly underinsured—even before we talk about umbrella insurance.

Who Should Absolutely Have Umbrella Insurance?

If you're an engineer and meet *any* of the following, get a quote:

- Net worth over $500,000

- Annual income over $100,000
- Own a home
- Have kids or teen drivers
- Own rental property
- Have dogs, pools, or trampolines (seriously)
- Serve on a nonprofit board or HOA

Remember: The more you have, the more you have to *lose.*

Real-World Engineer Scenarios

Scenario 1: Liam, a 32-year-old software engineer

Liam drives a Tesla and commutes to his job. One rainy evening, he hydroplanes and collides with another car. The driver sues for $700,000. Liam's auto policy covers $250,000. His $1M umbrella covers the remaining $450,000. His assets are safe.

Scenario 2: Maria, a 48-year-old civil engineer

Maria owns a duplex she rents out. A tenant's guest trips on a broken step and suffers a major injury. They sue for $900,000. Her landlord policy covers $300,000. Her umbrella covers the rest.

Scenario 3: Devin, a 55-year-old engineering manager

Devin's teenage son gets into a major accident driving the family car. The damages exceed their auto policy by $600,000. The umbrella policy protects Devin's 401(k), brokerage account, and home equity.

How to Get Umbrella Insurance

1. **Talk to your current insurer**

- Most major insurers offer umbrella policies (State Farm, Allstate, Travelers, etc.)

1. **Make sure your auto/home liability limits meet minimums**

- $250K/$500K for auto
- $300K for homeowners

1. **Get quotes for $1M to $5M in umbrella coverage**

- You may be surprised how inexpensive it is

1. **Consider bundling**

- You may get discounts for bundling auto, home, and umbrella

1. **Review annually**

- As your income and net worth grow, increase your coverage

What Coverage Amount Should You Get?

- Start with $1 million
- Add more if you:
- Own multiple properties
- Have significant savings or brokerage investments
- Have high public exposure (media, board seats, online presence)

A good rule: Match your umbrella coverage to your *total* net worth + projected income for the next 5–10 years.

This isn't about paranoia. It's about planning.

Common Questions and Misconceptions

"Isn't this overkill?"

Not if you've built something worth protecting. Umbrella insurance is cheap compared to what's at risk.

"Can I just rely on my auto/home policies?"

Not if their limits are low. Most lawsuits exceed those limits easily.

"What if I don't have many assets now?"

They can go after *future* earnings in some states. This isn't just about today—it's about protecting your trajectory.

"Isn't this only for the ultra-wealthy?"

No. It's for anyone with something to lose—and that includes most mid-career engineers.

Encouragement

You're more capable than you think.

Umbrella insurance isn't complicated. It's logical. It's efficient. It's just another layer in your financial system—like a backup generator for your wealth.

And you know how to design systems that account for worst-case scenarios.

Takeaways

- Umbrella insurance adds an extra layer of liability protection
- It's affordable—usually $150–$300 per year per million dollars
- It protects your assets, future income, and peace of mind
- Essential if you own property, earn a high income, or have liability exposure

The smartest engineers don't just optimize returns.

They mitigate risks.

They protect the system.

They build wealth and guard it.

Chapter 35: Estate Planning Basics for Analytical Thinkers

Estate planning isn't about death.

It's about *control.*

Control over what happens to your money, your property, your children, your legacy, and your voice—when you're no longer here to explain things, manage them, or fix them.

As an engineer, you're wired to solve problems, prevent failure, and design efficient systems. Estate planning is no different. It's a way to build a system that functions when you can't. One that passes on your values, not just your valuables.

But let's be real: most engineers procrastinate on this.

Why?

- It's uncomfortable.
- It feels abstract or premature.
- And—perhaps most importantly—it's not urgent.

This chapter is here to change that.

Not by guilting you. Not by throwing legal jargon at you. But by laying out a clear, logical framework for estate planning—one that speaks to your analytical brain and practical mindset.

Because here's the truth: whether you're 25 or 65, if you've built something—assets, income, a business, a family—you need a plan.

Let's build one together.

What Is Estate Planning, Really?

Estate planning is the process of organizing your affairs so that:

- Your assets go where *you* want them to go
- Your family and loved ones are protected
- Someone can act on your behalf if you become incapacitated
- You minimize taxes, delays, and legal costs

It's not just for the ultra-wealthy. It's for anyone who:

- Owns a home
- Has a retirement account
- Has kids
- Is married or in a committed relationship
- Owns a business
- Cares about what happens to their money—or the people they love—after they're gone

Core Components of an Estate Plan

1. **Will**
2. **Durable Power of Attorney (POA)**
3. **Healthcare Directive / Living Will**
4. **Revocable Living Trust** (optional but powerful)
5. **Beneficiary Designations**
6. **Letter of Intent or Instruction**

Let's walk through each—what it does, why it matters, and how to make it work.

1. The Will – Your Instruction Manual for Your Assets
2. A will is a legal document that states:

- Who gets what when you die
- Who will take care of your children (guardian)
- Who will manage the process (executor)

Without a will:

- The state decides who gets your assets
- A judge decides who raises your kids
- The process is longer, costlier, and more stressful for your family

What engineers should consider:

- Be specific and logical in assigning assets
- Choose an executor who's responsible, not just closest to you
- Review and update after major life changes (marriage, divorce, children, relocation)

Action Step:

If you have no will, schedule time this month to create one—either through an estate attorney or a reputable online service.

1. Durable Power of Attorney (POA)
2. A POA lets someone act on your behalf for financial matters if you're incapacitated.

That includes:

- Paying bills
- Managing investments
- Accessing bank accounts
- Filing taxes

Why it matters:

Without a POA, no one—not even your spouse—can legally act for you. They'd have to go to court for guardianship.

Engineers often choose:

- A spouse, sibling, or trusted adult child
- Someone with good judgment and attention to detail

You can make the POA effective immediately or only upon incapacity (springing).

Action Step:

Add a POA to your estate plan and make sure your bank or brokerage accepts it.

1. Healthcare Directive and HIPAA Authorization
2. This document does two things:

- States your wishes for medical care if you can't speak for yourself (life support, feeding tubes, etc.)
- Appoints a healthcare proxy to make decisions for you

Also include a HIPAA authorization form:

- Allows doctors to share your medical info with the people you trust

Why it matters:

- Prevents family conflict in medical emergencies
- Ensures your preferences are honored

Action Step:

Create your healthcare directive and give copies to your proxy and physician.

1. Revocable Living Trust – Optional but Smart
2. A living trust is a legal entity that holds your assets while you're alive and distributes them after your death, *without* going through probate.

Key advantages:

- Avoids probate court (which can be expensive and time-consuming)
- Keeps your affairs private (wills are public record)
- Allows faster access to assets for your heirs
- Gives more control over how and when assets are distributed

Who needs one?

- Anyone with over $100K in non-retirement assets
- Anyone who owns property in multiple states
- Blended families or second marriages
- People who want to control *how* heirs receive assets (e.g., staggered over time)

Drawbacks:

- More work up front (you have to transfer assets into the trust)
- More cost (legal fees for setup)

But for analytical thinkers? It's often worth it.

Action Step:

If your net worth is over $500K or your family situation is complex, talk to an estate attorney about a living trust.

1. Beneficiary Designations – The "Hidden Estate Plan"
2. Some assets don't follow your will. They pass automatically to whoever is listed as the beneficiary.

That includes:

- 401(k)s
- IRAs
- Life insurance
- HSAs
- Annuities

If you don't update these, your ex-spouse, estranged sibling, or outdated choice might receive a windfall.

Action Step:

Review all beneficiary forms annually or after major life events.

1. Letter of Intent or Instruction
2. This is not a legal document. But it's one of the most important.

It's a letter you write to your executor or family that includes:

- Your funeral or memorial wishes
- Account passwords and locations
- Digital assets (emails, photos, crypto keys)
- Instructions about pets, subscriptions, memberships, etc.

Think of it as the README file for your life.

Use a cloud-based password manager, encrypted files, or a printed packet in a fireproof safe.

Action Step:

Write your first draft of a letter of instruction. Keep it updated annually.

Estate Planning and Taxes – A Brief Primer

For most people, estate taxes aren't a concern.

- As of 2025, the federal estate tax exemption is over $13 million per person ($26M for couples)

But that could change.

- Some states have their own estate or inheritance taxes

If your net worth is approaching 7 or 8 figures:

- Consider irrevocable trusts, gifting strategies, or family limited partnerships
- Work with an estate attorney and financial advisor

Advanced Planning for Engineers

If you love system design, there's plenty to explore:

- Dynasty trusts for multi-generational wealth
- Charitable remainder trusts
- Grantor retained annuity trusts (GRATs)
- Asset protection trusts
- Qualified personal residence trusts (QPRTs)

You don't need to master them all.

Just know they exist—and get help when the system gets complex.

Common Misconceptions

"I'm young, I don't need this."

- If you're over 18, you need a POA and healthcare directive
- If you have kids or assets, you need a will

"My spouse will automatically get everything."

- Maybe. But not always. It depends on titling, state law, and beneficiary forms

"I don't have enough money to need a trust."

- Trusts aren't just for the ultra-wealthy—they're for people who want privacy, speed, and control

"It's too complicated."

- That's what lawyers and planners are for. You don't need to DIY the whole thing.

Encouragement

You're more capable than you think.

Estate planning isn't about being morbid. It's about being intentional.

You've worked hard to build your life. Estate planning is how you protect it—for yourself, and for the people you care about.

It's not about documents. It's about peace of mind.

Takeaways

- Every engineer needs at least a will, POA, and healthcare directive
- Review beneficiaries, titles, and account ownership regularly
- Trusts offer privacy, speed, and customization for those with complex needs
- Estate planning is a system—design it with intention

The smartest engineers don't just accumulate assets.

They plan for what happens next.

They think ahead.

They build systems that last.

Part VIII – Engineering Your Assets: Advanced Wealth Building

Part VIII is where the technical meets the tactical—where engineers turn solid foundations into scalable systems of wealth. By now, you've learned how to protect what you've built and structure your financial life with intention. This next section is about optimization: how to make your money not just work harder, but work smarter within a framework that fits your goals.

In this part of the book, we explore advanced wealth-building strategies through the lens of engineering logic. We'll break down complex concepts like tax-efficient investing, real estate leverage, Roth conversion timing, asset location, and income layering into straightforward, practical tools. We'll explore how engineers can use their analytical strengths to vet alternative investments, evaluate risk-adjusted returns, and design a multi-decade investment system that doesn't rely on guesswork or hype.

Whether you're a mid-career professional wondering if you're behind, or a seasoned engineer optimizing for early retirement or legacy planning, this section meets you where you are. With clear examples, formulas, and case studies rooted in real-life engineering challenges, you'll see how to model your wealth-building process the way you would approach any other technical system: with clarity, control, feedback loops, and continuous improvement.

Because the smartest engineers don't chase money—they engineer it.

Chapter 36: Real Estate Investing for Engineers

Let's start with a premise: Real estate investing isn't magic. It's a system.

And as an engineer, you already know how to model systems.

This chapter isn't about hyped-up guru advice or promises of passive income with zero effort. It's about understanding real estate as a *tool*—a powerful, capital-intensive, risk-adjusted tool for building wealth over time.

And like any tool, it needs to be selected, calibrated, and managed carefully.

So whether you're a 28-year-old software engineer curious about buying your first rental, a 40-year-old electrical engineer debating between real estate and index funds, or a 55-year-old who's owned a few properties but never run them like a business—this chapter is for you.

Let's break it down.

Why Real Estate Appeals to Engineers

Real estate appeals to logical thinkers for good reason:

- Tangibility – You can see it, touch it, and measure its cash flow
- Leverage – You can control large assets with relatively small capital
- Tax benefits – Real estate comes with depreciation, deductions, and 1031 exchanges
- Predictable inputs – Rent, expenses, and property value can be modeled

- Multiple return streams – Appreciation, cash flow, principal paydown, and tax shelter

And yet, most engineers overanalyze real estate until they're stuck in paralysis—or they jump in without modeling the risk.

This chapter will help you avoid both extremes.

Three Pillars of Real Estate Wealth

When you invest in real estate, your return comes from three primary sources:

1. **Cash Flow** – Monthly income after all expenses
2. **Appreciation** – Long-term increase in property value
3. **Tax Benefits** – Depreciation, write-offs, and capital gains deferral

Bonus: **Principal Paydown** – Your tenants pay down your mortgage each month, slowly increasing your equity

The right property delivers a blend of all four.

The wrong property destroys all four.

Let's talk about how to evaluate, select, and operate real estate as an engineer—not a speculator.

Buy-and-Hold Rental Real Estate – The Core Strategy

Buy-and-hold means you purchase property and rent it out for years or decades.

You make money through:

- Monthly rental income
- Long-term appreciation
- Tax deductions and depreciation

You can do this with:

- Single-family homes
- Duplexes, triplexes, or fourplexes (residential)

- Small apartment buildings (5+ units = commercial lending)

What matters most isn't the *type* of property.

It's the *numbers.*

Key Metrics Every Engineer Should Know

1. Cap Rate (Capitalization Rate)

Cap rate = Net Operating Income (NOI) / Purchase Price

NOI = Gross rents – operating expenses (excluding mortgage)

If a property earns $15,000/year in NOI and costs $300,000, the cap rate is 5%.

Cap rate gives you a sense of *unleveraged return.*

2. Cash-on-Cash Return

Cash-on-cash = (Annual pre-tax cash flow) / (Cash invested)

If you put $50K down on a property and earn $5K/year after expenses and mortgage, your cash-on-cash return is 10%.

This metric matters most to most investors—it tells you how hard your money is working.

3. Debt Coverage Ratio (DCR)

DCR = NOI / Annual Debt Service

A DCR of 1.25 means the property generates 25% more than your debt payments. Lenders typically want to see DCRs over 1.2.

4. Break-Even Rent

This is the monthly rent you need to cover mortgage, taxes, insurance, and expenses.

Knowing this number helps you set floor rents, model risk, and stress test vacancy.

5. Internal Rate of Return (IRR)

The IRR models total return over time, including appreciation, tax benefits, and final sale. It's complex—but engineers can model it in Excel or with REI software.

How to Find a Good Market

You don't have to buy in your backyard.

In fact, many engineers invest out of state.

Look for markets with:

- Population and job growth
- Landlord-friendly laws
- Solid rent-to-price ratios (1% rule is a rough guide)
- Diverse employment base (not one employer or industry)

Avoid markets that are:

- Overheated and unaffordable
- Dependent on one economic driver (oil, tourism, etc.)
- Highly regulated or anti-landlord

Use data:

- Zillow Rent Index
- Redfin, Realtor.com trends
- Roofstock, Mashvisor, or BiggerPockets Market Finder tools

Buying Your First Rental Property – Step by Step

1. **Define your strategy** – Cash flow? Appreciation? Long-term hold?
2. **Set your budget** – How much can you invest without disrupting your primary goals?
3. **Get pre-approved** – Residential (1–4 units) loans are based on your income and credit
4. **Build your team** – Agent, lender, property manager, insurance broker, CPA
5. **Analyze deals weekly** – Use a spreadsheet or property calculator
6. **Make offers and negotiate** – Your agent will guide this
7. **Inspect thoroughly** – Use pros. Don't skip this.
8. **Close and take possession** – Make sure insurance and utilities are in place

9. **Rent it out** – Screen tenants carefully or hire a property manager
10. **Monitor and improve** – Track expenses, cash flow, and maintenance

Financing Options

- **Conventional Loans** – 20–25% down, best rates
- **Portfolio Loans** – Held by small banks, flexible underwriting
- **DSCR Loans** – Based on property cash flow, not your income
- **HELOC or Cash-Out Refi** – Pull equity from your home to buy
- **Partnerships** – Team up with another investor (use a written agreement!)

Self-Managing vs. Hiring a Property Manager

Self-Managing

Pros:

- Higher margins
- Full control
- Learn the business inside and out

Cons:

- Time-consuming
- Can be emotional or stressful
- Risk of burnout or costly mistakes

Using a Property Manager

Pros:

- Hands-off
- Professional tenant screening and systems
- Scalable

Cons:

- Typically 8%–10% of monthly rent
- Less control over decisions

Most engineers with full-time jobs eventually outsource management. Just choose wisely—interview 3–5 companies.

Common Real Estate Investment Mistakes

- Underestimating expenses (especially CapEx)
- Overleveraging with adjustable-rate mortgages
- Buying for appreciation instead of cash flow
- Not screening tenants properly
- Forgetting vacancy, maintenance, and turnover costs

What About REITs and Real Estate Funds?

If you want real estate exposure without the hassle of owning property, consider:

- **Public REITs** – Like stocks, traded on exchanges, highly liquid
- **Private REITs** – Less liquid, potentially higher returns, higher fees
- **Crowdfunded Real Estate** – Sites like Fundrise, RealtyMogul
- **Real Estate ETFs** – VNQ, SCHH, etc.

These options:

- Don't use leverage
- Don't offer direct tax benefits (no depreciation to you)
- Are passive and diversified

Real Estate vs. Stock Market – Which Is Better?

There's no universal answer.

Real estate offers:

- Control
- Leverage
- Tangible asset
- Tax shelter

But it requires:

- Time
- Capital
- Risk tolerance
- Management

Stocks offer:

- Liquidity
- Simplicity
- Diversification
- Easy automation

But they expose you to:

- Market volatility
- Emotional investing
- Lower tax efficiency if held outside retirement accounts

Many engineers do both: invest passively in the market and use real estate to accelerate or diversify wealth.

Advanced Topics for Engineers Who Want More

- 1031 exchanges to defer capital gains
- Cost segregation to accelerate depreciation
- BRRRR strategy (Buy, Rehab, Rent, Refinance, Repeat)
- Multifamily syndications

- Opportunity Zones
- Tax strategies with real estate professional status

Encouragement

You're more capable than you think.

Real estate isn't about luck. It's about systems.

You've already built models, optimized processes, and solved for constraints in your career. This is no different. The math works if you do.

Don't buy based on emotion.

Don't overanalyze forever.

Pick a strategy.

Run the numbers.

Start small.

Iterate.

Takeaways

- Real estate can be a powerful wealth-building tool for engineers
- Understand the metrics: cap rate, cash-on-cash, DCR, IRR
- Run the numbers like a system—not a gamble
- Start with small, cash-flowing properties in good markets
- Use leverage wisely and manage risk with reserves
- Decide early: active landlord or passive investor?

The smartest engineers don't speculate.

They evaluate.

They structure.

They engineer wealth with intention.

Chapter 37: Business Ownership vs. Being an Employee

For engineers, the question of whether to stay on the traditional employee path or take the leap into business ownership is both exhilarating and intimidating. It's a decision packed with layers—financial, emotional, logistical, and strategic.

And because engineers often think in systems, processes, and models, this isn't just about income. It's about *control.* It's about *design.* It's about the kind of life you want to engineer—not just for your career, but for your finances, your time, your family, and your impact.

This chapter is here to unpack the trade-offs, the math, the mindset, and the mechanics of business ownership versus being an employee—from the lens of an engineer who wants to make intentional decisions, not emotional ones.

The Core Trade-Off: Security vs. Autonomy

At the heart of this decision is a trade-off:

- Employees trade control for stability
- Business owners trade stability for control

Neither is right or wrong. But they produce very different outcomes over time.

Being an Employee – The Upside

Let's start with the case for staying employed.

As an engineer working for a company, you get:

- A steady paycheck
- Benefits (health insurance, retirement plans, paid time off)
- Predictable work hours
- Clear job responsibilities
- Career progression paths

This system is especially attractive when you're starting out, supporting a family, or don't want to blur the line between your profession and your income.

And with some strategic moves, it can be very financially rewarding:

- Maximize 401(k) and HSA contributions
- Earn bonuses and stock options
- Negotiate for raises, promotions, or flexibility
- Invest surplus income in real estate or markets

Risks of Being an Employee

- You're reliant on one income stream (your job)
- Layoffs, downsizing, or corporate pivots are out of your control
- Salary increases may slow as you progress
- Equity upside is capped (unless you're in early-stage startups)
- Your schedule and lifestyle are partly dictated by someone else

Some engineers are fine with that. Others aren't.

The Case for Business Ownership

Being a business owner means you:

- Control your income potential
- Decide who you work with and what you work on
- Build something with equity that can grow or be sold

- Create tax-advantaged income and wealth
- Design your own systems, processes, and schedule

It's not easy. But it's not impossible either—especially for engineers who:

- Think logically
- Excel at problem solving
- Can build scalable products or services
- Are willing to learn sales, marketing, and financial strategy

Types of Engineer-Owned Businesses

1. **Consulting or Freelance Services** – Contract work for clients
2. **Product-Based Companies** – Build and sell software, tools, or physical products
3. **Agencies** – Technical recruiting, IT services, automation consulting
4. **Real Estate Businesses** – Rentals, syndications, flipping, development
5. **Content/Education Businesses** – Courses, YouTube, newsletters
6. **Tech Startups** – Scalable products, often with investor capital

Each has different startup costs, risk profiles, and scalability.

The Financial Model of Business Ownership

Let's break down what you need to model:

- Startup costs
- Operating expenses
- Time to first dollar
- Customer acquisition cost (CAC)
- Revenue per customer
- Lifetime value (LTV)
- Burn rate and runway
- Tax strategy (S-Corp, LLC, solo 401(k), etc.)

Most new businesses don't turn a meaningful profit in year one. That's normal. You're building infrastructure.

You'll also face more complex tax filing, irregular income, and the need for self-funded benefits.

But the upside?

- You keep the profit
- You write off legitimate expenses
- You can structure income to reduce taxes
- You build an asset that can be sold or inherited

Tax Differences: Employee vs. Owner

As an employee:

- W-2 income is fully taxed (federal, state, payroll)
- Limited deductions
- Access to 401(k), HSA

As a business owner:

- Pay yourself a reasonable salary and take the rest as distributions (less payroll tax)
- Deduct business expenses (home office, travel, equipment, education)
- Choose optimal entity structure (LLC, S-Corp, etc.)
- Contribute to solo 401(k), SEP IRA, or defined benefit plan

Decision Matrix: What to Consider

1. **Risk Tolerance** – Can you handle income variability?
2. **Time Horizon** – Are you in this for long-term equity or short-term cash?
3. **Family and Lifestyle Needs** – How much flexibility vs. structure do you want?

4. **Health Benefits** – Can you find affordable coverage independently?
5. **Income Needs** – Do you need to match or exceed your current salary quickly?
6. **Skill Set** – Are you willing to sell, market, and lead?
7. **Exit Strategy** – Is this a business you'll sell, scale, or shut down?

Real Engineer Examples

Raj, 33, Mechanical Engineer

Raj launched a niche product development firm. First year: $42K income. Year five: $310K, four contractors, two patents.

Elena, 41, Civil Engineer

Elena stayed employed but started buying small multifamily rentals. Now owns 12 units producing $65K net annually.

Tyler, 27, Software Engineer

Tyler freelanced nights and weekends, saved $80K, and launched a SaaS tool. Two years in: $12K/month recurring revenue.

Brian, 52, Electrical Engineer

Brian stayed in his role and negotiated sabbaticals every 5 years. He never wanted to be an entrepreneur—but he built a portfolio and FIRE'd at 56.

Hybrid Paths

You don't have to choose one or the other.

Many engineers:

- Freelance while working full-time
- Consult part-time and teach part-time
- Launch side businesses or real estate investments
- Negotiate 4-day weeks to explore ventures

This hybrid model offers:

- Income stability
- Experimentation runway
- Optionality

But it requires careful time management, clear boundaries, and sometimes, disclosure to your employer.

Action Steps for Either Path

If staying employed:

- Max out employer benefits
- Ask for raises proactively
- Learn to negotiate salary and equity
- Automate investing
- Build side income streams

If exploring ownership:

- Start small—don't quit yet
- Define a business model (what problem do you solve?)
- Track startup costs and projected revenue
- Form a legal entity
- Open a business bank account
- Get accounting help early

Encouragement

You're more capable than you think.

Whether you stay an employee, become an entrepreneur, or blend both—what matters most is *intentionality.*

Don't drift through your career.

Design it.

Run the numbers. Map the trade-offs. Think like an engineer. And most of all—build the system that gets you where you want to go.

Takeaways

- Employment offers stability and benefits; ownership offers control and equity
- Real estate, consulting, and content businesses can all be engineered

for cash flow
- Business ownership has tax advantages but requires more planning and risk tolerance
- Hybrid approaches are viable and often ideal for engineers
- Your career is your greatest asset—whether you scale it or own it, treat it like a system

The smartest engineers don't just follow a career path.

They design one.

Chapter 38: Alternative Investments – Private Equity, Angel Investing, Crowdfunding

When most people think of investing, they think of stocks, bonds, mutual funds, maybe real estate.

But there's a whole other category of assets that don't live on your typical brokerage platform—yet are increasingly becoming part of the conversation for high-income professionals, including engineers.

These are called *alternative investments*, or "alts."

They include things like:

- Private equity
- Venture capital
- Angel investing
- Real estate crowdfunding
- Private credit
- Hedge funds
- Collectibles, crypto, and more

This chapter focuses on three key areas where analytical, high-earning engineers often find themselves curious: private equity, angel investing, and crowdfunding.

We'll walk through what they are, how they work, what risks and returns to expect, and how to approach them with logic, not hype.

Because alternatives aren't just edgy. They're opaque. They're illiquid. They're exciting—and dangerous if misunderstood.

But if used thoughtfully, they can be powerful tools for long-term wealth building.

What Are Alternative Investments, Exactly?

Alternative investments are any investments *outside* of public markets.

That means:

- They're not traded on exchanges
- They're often illiquid
- They may have higher minimums or be limited to accredited investors
- They're typically harder to value

Why do investors pursue them?

- Potential for higher returns
- Diversification from public market volatility
- Access to unique deals and emerging industries

But those come with trade-offs:

- Less transparency
- Less regulation
- Longer time horizons
- Higher fees

Let's break down the big three.

Private Equity – Owning Parts of Private Companies

Private equity (PE) is the practice of investing in private businesses that are not publicly traded.

This can include:

- Buyouts of existing businesses

- Growth capital for scaling companies
- Turnaround of distressed businesses
- Venture-style investments with later-stage companies

PE firms usually raise large funds from institutional and high-net-worth investors, buy companies, improve them operationally or financially, and sell them 3–10 years later for a profit.

As an individual investor, your access to PE depends on:

- Net worth and income (you may need to be accredited)
- Your network and exposure to deal flow
- Platforms that offer PE fund access (like Fundrise, Moonfare, or direct offerings)

Pros:

- Potentially high returns (often 10%–20% IRR)
- Access to non-correlated assets
- Equity ownership in tangible businesses

Cons:

- Illiquidity (capital is locked up for 7–10 years)
- High minimums (sometimes $250K+)
- High fees (2 and 20 models are common)
- Risk of total capital loss

What to look for:

- Experienced management teams
- Clear operating model and exit strategy
- Aligned incentives (GP co-investment)

Engineers who succeed in private equity investing often:

- Know the sector well (tech, biotech, energy, etc.)
- Have direct access to operators or sponsors
- Understand due diligence and deal terms

Angel Investing – Betting Early, Betting Small

Angel investing means providing early-stage capital to startups—typically in exchange for convertible debt or equity.

It's the riskiest of the three categories.

Roughly 9 out of 10 startups fail. But the one that wins can win *big.*

Angel investing appeals to engineers because:

- You understand the tech or product
- You like innovation
- You want to support ideas and founders
- You can write small checks ($1K–$25K)

The mechanics:

- Startups raise pre-seed, seed, or Series A capital
- Angels provide funds in SAFEs, convertible notes, or equity rounds
- Exit may take 5–10 years (via acquisition or IPO)

Minimums:

- As low as $100 via crowdfunding
- $1K–$10K is typical on platforms like AngelList, Republic, WeFunder, or SeedInvest

Pros:

- Early access to groundbreaking tech

- Asymmetric upside potential
- Founders often accessible and mission-driven

Cons:

- High risk of total loss
- Illiquid and unregulated
- Due diligence is often thin
- Success takes years (if it comes at all)

How to do it smartly:

- Diversify (20+ small investments > 2 large bets)
- Co-invest with experienced angels or syndicates
- Look for traction, not just ideas
- Back founders, not just business models
- Only use money you can afford to lose

Real Estate Crowdfunding – Fractional Ownership Without the Hassle

If you want real estate exposure without buying entire buildings or becoming a landlord, crowdfunding is an accessible gateway.

You can invest in:

- Residential or commercial properties
- Development deals
- Real estate debt (private lending)

Platforms include:

- Fundrise
- RealtyMogul
- Crowdstreet
- Groundfloor

- Roofstock One

Minimums range from $10 to $25,000, depending on the platform and deal.

Pros:

- Real estate exposure with lower capital
- Passive and diversified
- Some offer monthly or quarterly distributions

Cons:

- Platform risk
- Limited liquidity (some have 3–5 year lockups)
- Lower control and transparency
- Fees may be hidden

How it works:

- Choose a fund (eREIT) or direct deal
- Invest via ACH or wire
- Receive reports and distributions (if applicable)
- Exit after hold period or via secondary market (if offered)

Due diligence tips:

- Read offering memorandums carefully
- Compare platforms' historical returns and track records
- Look for audited financials and SEC compliance

Alternative Investing Strategy for Engineers

If you're considering alternatives, treat them like an engineering project:

1. **Define your objective**

- Are you seeking yield? Diversification? Asymmetric upside?

1. **Quantify your risk tolerance**

- What % of your net worth are you willing to lose?

1. **Build your system**

- Diversify across asset types and time horizons
- Use a spreadsheet or dashboard to track performance and liquidity

1. **Allocate intentionally**

- Public markets: 60%–80%
- Real estate: 10%–20%
- Alternatives: 5%–15%

1. **Revisit and rebalance**

- Annual reviews
- Document lessons learned from each deal

Red Flags to Avoid

- Promises of guaranteed returns
- Complex structures you don't understand
- High-pressure timelines or exclusivity language
- Lack of audited financials
- Unclear exit strategies

The Regulatory Side – Who Can Invest?

Many alts require you to be an accredited investor:

- $200K+ income ($300K with spouse) *or*
- $1M+ net worth (excluding primary residence)

Some platforms offer access to non-accredited investors, but with more limits.

Always consult your CPA or legal advisor before making private investments.

Real-World Engineer Scenarios

Jason, 39, Software Engineer

Jason joins an AngelList syndicate and invests $5K into a pre-seed AI startup. Seven years later, the company is acquired for 20x.

Maya, 44, Structural Engineer

Maya uses Fundrise to invest $50K in diversified eREITs. It pays 6.5% annually and offers quarterly liquidity.

Devin, 36, Electrical Engineer

Devin joins a local angel network and co-invests in 12 startups over 4 years. Two fail, six break even, four are still active. One is raising a Series C with 12x markup.

Encouragement

You're more capable than you think.

Alternative investments are not just for venture capitalists or insiders. But they *do* require thought, discipline, and education.

Don't dive in without a plan.

Don't chase shiny objects.

Don't allocate more than you can afford to lose.

But *do* explore them.

Because as you accumulate wealth, your job isn't just to grow it.

It's to build an investment system that reflects your vision, values, and risk profile.

Takeaways

- Private equity, angel investing, and crowdfunding can diversify and grow wealth
- These investments are illiquid, risky, and require due diligence
- Engineers should apply analytical rigor: model returns, understand fees, evaluate teams
- Use alternatives to complement, not replace, a solid core portfolio

The smartest engineers don't chase trends.

They study systems.

They test, refine, and optimize their portfolio like any other complex model.

Chapter 39: Venture Capital – What Engineers Need to Know Before Jumping In

If you're an engineer, odds are you've crossed paths with venture capital. Maybe you've worked at a startup backed by VCs. Maybe friends have pitched you on "the next big thing." Maybe you've even considered launching your own company—or joining one early.

Either way, venture capital (VC) sits at the intersection of innovation and investment. It's exhilarating. It's risky. It's misunderstood. And if you're thinking of getting involved—as a founder, investor, employee, or advisor—you need to understand the rules of the game.

This chapter unpacks VC with clarity, structure, and relevance—for engineers who think in models and systems, not hype.

Because VC isn't just about unicorns. It's about capital structure, exit math, dilution risk, and power dynamics. And the sooner you grasp that, the more equipped you'll be to navigate it.

Let's walk through what venture capital is, how it works, and what you need to know—before you jump in.

What Is Venture Capital?

Venture capital is a form of private equity financing that invests in high-growth startups with the potential for large returns.

It's called *venture* capital because the outcomes are uncertain. Most bets fail. But the few that win can generate 10x, 50x, or 100x returns.

VC funds raise money from limited partners (LPs)—like pensions, endowments, and high-net-worth individuals—and invest that capital into startups.

They typically:

- Take equity in exchange for capital
- Join the board or get observer rights
- Expect an exit in 5–10 years (via IPO or acquisition)

VC investing is:

- Illiquid
- High risk
- Long term
- Asymmetric (huge upside, many failures)

Engineers should think of VC like an experimental portfolio:

- 1 or 2 companies will return the entire fund
- 3 to 5 may break even or do OK
- The rest will fail or return little

How Venture Capital Funds Work

A typical VC fund has a structure like this:

- **GP (General Partner)** – The VC firm that manages the fund
- **LPs (Limited Partners)** – Investors who provide capital
- **Fund Size** – Ranges from $10M to $1B+
- **Fees** – Typically 2% management + 20% carry (profit share)

The fund has a 10-year life:

- Years 1–3: Invest in startups
- Years 4–10: Manage, grow, and exit the portfolio

VCs want to:

- Invest early (seed to Series A)
- Add value (advice, networks, recruiting)
- Exit via acquisition or IPO

Stages of VC Investment

1. **Pre-seed** – Idea stage, small checks ($25K–$250K)
2. **Seed** – MVP, early traction ($500K–$2M)
3. **Series A** – Product-market fit, growth plans ($2M–$15M)
4. **Series B/C/D** – Scaling, expansion, large teams ($15M+)
5. **Exit** – IPO, acquisition, or failure

Each round dilutes previous investors but (hopefully) increases valuation.

Dilution and Cap Tables – Understand the Math

Let's say you join a startup and get 1% equity.

That sounds great—until you realize:

- It's 1% *pre-dilution*
- Each new funding round dilutes you unless you have pro-rata rights (rare for employees)
- By the time the company exits, your 1% may be 0.25%

So what matters?

- **Valuation** – What price the investors pay
- **Option pool** – Set aside for employees; often dilutive
- **Vesting** – How long until your shares are fully yours (usually 4 years)
- **Exit terms** – Are there liquidation preferences, participating preferred shares, or seniority?

Engineers should model cap tables to understand the real-world impact of dilution.

Equity vs. Salary – Know Your Value

If you're offered a startup job:

- Compare base salary to market rates
- Ask about cash vs. equity mix
- Review the option grant, strike price, and vesting schedule
- Ask if options are ISOs or NSOs (tax differences)
- Consider early exercise rights (and their tax consequences)

Rule of thumb: Only accept below-market cash if you believe the equity has outsized potential and you're aligned with the mission.

Be realistic:

- Most startups fail
- Your equity could be worth $0
- But if it wins, even a small stake could change your life

Founding a Startup – What Engineers Often Overlook

VC-backed entrepreneurship is not like bootstrapping.

It's:

- Fast-paced
- Growth-obsessed
- Capital-intensive
- Outcome-driven

You'll need to:

- Pitch VCs with a big vision
- Give up significant ownership
- Hire fast, spend fast, iterate fast
- Accept dilution and board oversight

Trade-offs:

- VC money accelerates—but also dictates—your path
- You may end up owning 10% or less of your own company at exit

That's fine *if* the pie is big enough.

But you need to model it:

- What is a realistic exit value?
- What's your ownership stake then?
- What's your tax treatment?

VC isn't free money—it's a partnership with expectations.

How Engineers Can Invest in Venture Capital

If you want to become a VC investor yourself, there are a few paths:

1. **Join a VC Firm**

- Roles include analyst, associate, principal, partner
- Requires sourcing deals, due diligence, thesis-building

1. **Invest via Syndicates**

- AngelList, Jason Calacanis, etc.
- You back other angels or VCs with small checks

1. **Start Your Own Fund or SPV**

- Pool capital and invest in startups
- Requires legal setup, investor management, and deal access

1. **Back Founders Directly**

- Via SAFE or convertible note
- Often relationship-based

Investor Considerations:

- Are you accredited?
- Can you afford to lock up this capital for 7–10 years?
- How will you do due diligence?
- What's your sector expertise or competitive edge?

What Engineers Bring to VC

VCs like engineers because you can:

- Understand technical products
- Vet founders from a product and market perspective
- Spot BS in pitches
- Help with product, recruiting, scaling

But to succeed, you also need:

- Strong network for sourcing deals
- Emotional resilience to handle failure
- Storytelling and fundraising skills (if raising a fund)
- Portfolio thinking (diversify your bets)

VC Red Flags and Risks

- Chasing unicorns without diligence
- Overweighting one deal
- Conflicts of interest (advising and investing)
- Joining cap tables without understanding terms
- Neglecting taxes (QSBS, AMT, phantom income)

Tax Considerations

- **Qualified Small Business Stock (QSBS)** – Potentially $10M+ capital gains exclusion if held 5+ years
- **Incentive Stock Options (ISOs)** – Favorable treatment if held long enough, but may trigger AMT
- **Convertible notes and SAFEs** – Taxable when converted, not when invested

Always consult a CPA who understands startup equity.

Encouragement

You're more capable than you think.

Whether you're investing, advising, joining, or founding—you bring a rare blend of technical insight and analytical rigor.

Just don't confuse enthusiasm for experience.

Don't let fear of missing out override financial fundamentals.

Don't jump in without understanding the system you're entering.

Takeaways

- VC is about asymmetric upside, but with high failure rates
- Engineers must understand cap tables, dilution, and equity terms
- VC-backed startups grow fast but often sacrifice control and profitability
- You can invest in VC as an angel, LP, or syndicate member—but only with capital you can afford to lose

The smartest engineers don't blindly follow trends.

They model, monitor, and iterate—just like they do with any complex system.

Chapter 40: Protecting Wealth Through Asset Diversification

Let's begin with a simple engineering analogy: You wouldn't design a critical system with a single point of failure. You'd introduce redundancy, backups, and buffers.

The same logic applies to your finances.

Diversification is financial risk management in its purest form. It doesn't guarantee returns. But it reduces the chances that one bad decision, one asset class, or one market cycle derails your entire financial plan.

For engineers, diversification isn't just a buzzword—it's a structural principle. And when applied deliberately, it becomes one of the most powerful tools to protect and grow your wealth over time.

This chapter will walk you through diversification at every level: asset classes, accounts, time horizons, income sources, and even geography. We'll break down what diversification really means, what it doesn't, and how to apply it without overcomplicating your strategy.

Diversification: The Core Idea

At its core, diversification means spreading your investments so that a failure or downturn in one area doesn't take down the whole system.

It's not about maximizing return.

It's about optimizing *risk-adjusted* return.

In engineering terms: it's increasing system stability through modular redundancy and variance dampening.

Where Diversification Matters

Diversification isn't just about owning some stocks and some bonds. It spans multiple dimensions:

1. Asset Class Diversification
2. Sector Diversification
3. Geographic Diversification
4. Account Type Diversification
5. Time Horizon Diversification
6. Income Stream Diversification

Let's break each one down.

1. Asset Class Diversification
2. This is the most basic form of diversification.

You don't want all your money in:

- Just stocks
- Just crypto
- Just real estate
- Just cash

A solid portfolio might include:

- Domestic stocks (large-cap, mid-cap, small-cap)
- International stocks (developed and emerging markets)
- Bonds (treasuries, corporate, municipal)
- Real estate (REITs or direct holdings)
- Cash and cash equivalents (high-yield savings, T-bills)
- Alternatives (private equity, venture capital, commodities, crypto)

Each asset class behaves differently across market cycles. When one zigs, another may zag.

1. Sector Diversification
2. Even within stocks, avoid overconcentration.

Owning five tech stocks is not diversification.
A diversified stock portfolio includes multiple sectors:

- Technology
- Healthcare
- Industrials
- Energy
- Consumer staples
- Financials
- Utilities

Consider using broad-based index funds or ETFs that spread across sectors.

1. Geographic Diversification
2. Don't bet your entire future on one country—even if it's the U.S.

International markets:

- Reduce home country bias
- Provide access to different economic cycles
- Hedge against currency and political risks

You can diversify globally through:

- International ETFs or mutual funds
- Global real estate holdings
- Foreign direct investments (if qualified)

1. Account Type Diversification
2. This is often overlooked.

Having money in different *types* of accounts gives you tax flexibility later.
Types include:

- Tax-deferred (401(k), traditional IRA)
- Tax-free (Roth IRA, Roth 401(k), HSA)
- Taxable (brokerage accounts, savings)

Why it matters:

- You can manage taxes in retirement
- You can withdraw from the most efficient account depending on your income
- You reduce exposure to future tax policy changes

1. Time Horizon Diversification
2. Different goals have different timelines.

You wouldn't invest your emergency fund in aggressive growth stocks.
Segment your money:

- Short-term (0–2 years): cash, money markets
- Medium-term (3–5 years): bonds, conservative ETFs
- Long-term (10+ years): stocks, real estate, alts

Matching your investments to your timeline ensures you're not forced to sell in a downturn.

1. Income Stream Diversification
2. This goes beyond investments.

It's about protecting your ability to earn.
Ways to diversify income:

- Salary from W-2 job
- Side business or consulting
- Rental income
- Dividends and interest
- Royalties or IP
- Social Security or pensions (later)

If one stream dries up, the others help you stay afloat.

Engineers who thrive financially often build multiple income streams—either passively or actively.

The Illusion of Diversification

Not all diversification is helpful.

If your portfolio has:

- Five tech ETFs
- Three rental properties in one city
- Two crypto coins that are highly correlated

You're not diversified. You're just *duplicated.*

Use tools like:

- Correlation matrices
- Beta analysis
- Factor exposure breakdowns

Diversification Isn't Set-and-Forget

Markets change. Your life changes. Tax laws change.

Revisit your allocations:

- Annually, or after big life events
- When your risk tolerance changes
- When market valuations shift significantly

Rebalancing helps keep your system aligned.

Example: If stocks boom and now make up 80% of your portfolio (vs. a target of 60%), rebalancing means selling some and reallocating to bonds, cash, or alts.

Don't chase returns—rebalance to manage risk.

Diversification and Taxes

Diversifying account types and asset locations can save you thousands. For example:

- Hold dividend-paying stocks in tax-advantaged accounts
- Use tax-loss harvesting in taxable accounts
- Don't hold high-turnover mutual funds in taxable accounts

Asset *location* matters almost as much as allocation.

Action Steps to Build Diversified Wealth

1. Run a full portfolio analysis – What % of your net worth is in each asset class?
2. Map your current and projected income streams
3. Identify concentration risks (e.g., too much employer stock)
4. Allocate across accounts (taxable, tax-free, tax-deferred)
5. Rebalance annually using set thresholds (e.g., 5% bands)
6. Consider real estate, small business, or alternative investments as side buckets—not core replacements
7. Use planning software or work with a fee-only advisor to model outcomes

Real Engineer Scenarios

Elena, 38, Civil Engineer

All her investments were in her 401(k), 100% U.S. growth stocks. During a downturn, she lost 27% and had no cash buffer.

Marcus, 44, Electrical Engineer

He diversified into rental properties, international index funds, and started a consulting side hustle. His portfolio stayed resilient during tech crashes.

Priya, 29, Software Engineer

She split her savings: 50% Roth IRA in a global index fund, 30% in a brokerage account with dividend stocks, and 20% in a Fundrise eREIT. She rebalances quarterly and tracks performance in a spreadsheet.

Encouragement

You're more capable than you think.

Diversification isn't glamorous. But it's foundational.

It's what keeps you steady when the market isn't.

It's what prevents one bad investment from derailing a lifetime of effort.

It's what turns your wealth into a *system*—not just a collection of bets.

Takeaways

- Diversification isn't just stocks and bonds—it's across asset types, timelines, taxes, and income streams
- Too much concentration increases risk—even in things you know well
- You can design your financial plan like a resilient system, not a brittle portfolio
- Rebalancing and tax-aware allocation are just as important as what you invest in

The smartest engineers don't chase fads.

They build stability.

They monitor feedback.

They adapt over time.

They diversify with intention.

Part IX – Preparing for Financial Independence

Part IX is where all your planning, modeling, and disciplined decision-making converge. This isn't just about retirement—it's about designing a life of freedom, control, and optionality. Whether you want to retire early, switch careers, start a business, or simply work on your own terms, this section is your blueprint.

Engineers don't stumble into financial independence—they model it. This part helps you run the simulations, stress test your assumptions, and make sure your systems will hold up over time. You'll learn how to calculate your FIRE number, create sustainable withdrawal strategies, and protect your wealth against inflation, taxes, market downturns, and healthcare surprises.

It's also about mindset. Because financial independence isn't just a number—it's a shift in how you think about time, purpose, and legacy. Part IX will help you transition from accumulation to optimization, from building to living, and from earning to engineering the life you truly want.

Chapter 41: Defining Your Financial Independence Number

When most people hear the phrase "financial independence," their mind drifts to retirement at age 65. Maybe they picture a golf course. Or a beach. Or, more realistically, not worrying about bills.

But for engineers—especially those who think in systems and long-range models—financial independence means something more precise, more intentional, and frankly, more empowering.

Financial independence is the point at which your investments, assets, and passive income streams can fully cover your living expenses for the rest of your life—without requiring you to work for money again.

It doesn't mean you stop working. It means you no longer *have* to work.

And the key to reaching that point? Knowing your number.

That's what this chapter is about: how to define, calculate, and refine your *Financial Independence Number*—the single most important benchmark in your personal wealth-building journey.

Because the truth is, if you don't define the target, you can't build a system to hit it.

What Is a Financial Independence Number?

Your Financial Independence (FI) Number is the amount of money you need invested to support your lifestyle indefinitely—assuming reasonable withdrawal rates and expected investment returns.

In math terms:

FI Number = Annual Spending × Withdrawal Rate Inverse

Example:

If you spend $80,000/year and plan to withdraw 4%, you need:

$80,000 ÷ 0.04 = $2,000,000

That's your FI number.

But as engineers, we can go far deeper than this surface-level estimate.

Understanding the 4% Rule (and Its Limitations)

The 4% rule comes from the Trinity Study, which analyzed historical market data to determine a "safe withdrawal rate" over 30-year retirement periods.

It concluded:

- If you withdraw 4% of your initial portfolio and adjust for inflation, there's a very high probability your money will last 30+ years.

But there are caveats:

- It assumes historical market performance
- It assumes a 50/50 stock-bond allocation
- It doesn't account for sequence of returns risk
- It ignores taxes, healthcare, and lifestyle changes

That's why defining your FI number requires more than multiplying by 25 (the inverse of 4%).

You need to engineer it.

Step 1: Define Your Target Annual Spending

Start with today's expenses, but adjust for:

- Kids moving out or going to college
- Mortgage payoff or downsizing
- Travel or hobbies in early retirement
- Healthcare costs pre- and post-Medicare
- Inflation over time

Create a base number:

- Essential expenses (housing, food, healthcare, taxes)
- Discretionary expenses (travel, hobbies, gifts)
- Contingency buffer (5% to 10%)

Let's say your analysis shows:

- Essentials: $55,000
- Discretionary: $25,000
- Buffer: $10,000
- = Total Annual Spending: $90,000

Step 2: Adjust for Inflation

Use your current age and expected retirement age to project your expenses in *future dollars.*

Formula:

Future Value = Present Value × (1 + inflation rate) ^ years

If you're 35 now and want to retire at 55 (20 years), and assume 2.5% inflation:

$90,000 × (1.025)^20 ≈ $147,636

Your FI target should support $147,636/year *in future dollars.*

Step 3: Determine Your Withdrawal Rate

This is where you build your model.

Conservative rates:

- 3.0% = very safe, allows for longer retirements and volatility
- 3.5% = reasonable for early retirees or high uncertainty
- 4.0% = traditional safe withdrawal estimate
- 4.5% = aggressive, assumes strong market returns

Let's assume 3.5%:

$147,636 ÷ 0.035 ≈ $4,218,171

That's your **inflation-adjusted FI number** at age 55.

Step 4: Back-Calculate How to Reach It

Now reverse-engineer how to get there.

Let's assume:

- You're 35 now
- You have $250,000 saved already
- You invest $3,000/month ($36,000/year)
- Your portfolio earns 6.5% average return (after inflation)

Use a future value calculator:

$FV = PV \times (1 + r)^n + PMT \times [((1 + r)^n - 1) \div r]$

This gives a projected portfolio of around $4.25M by age 55.

You're on track.

But what if you hit a bear market? Or need to retire early? That's where dynamic planning comes in.

Stress Testing Your FI Number

Engineers don't just build for ideal conditions.

They stress-test for edge cases.

Scenarios to model:

- Market crash in first 5 years of retirement
- Inflation runs at 4% instead of 2.5%
- You need $120,000/year instead of $90,000
- You work part-time for a few years (semi-retirement)
- You sell a business or receive a windfall

Use tools like:

- FIRECalc
- Portfolio Visualizer
- Personal Capital's retirement planner
- Your own Excel/Sheets models

The goal: Build a resilient plan that survives *bad years,* not just good ones.

The Role of Taxes in Your FI Number

Withdrawal strategy impacts taxes.

If all your money is in traditional 401(k)s and IRAs, withdrawals are taxed as ordinary income.

If you have Roth accounts, you can withdraw tax-free.

If you have brokerage accounts, you get capital gains treatment (which may be 0% if income is low).

So:

- Diversify account types (taxable, tax-deferred, tax-free)
- Create a Roth conversion plan (especially in low-income years)
- Use capital loss harvesting and asset location to reduce drag

Reaching your FI number is one thing.

Accessing it tax-efficiently is another.

Healthcare Considerations

Healthcare before Medicare is one of the biggest blind spots.

Options:

- ACA marketplace (subsidy planning is key)
- Health sharing ministries
- COBRA (temporary)
- Part-time jobs with benefits

Model in at least $15,000/year (per couple) for private insurance pre-Medicare.

After 65:

- Use Medicare + Medigap or Advantage plans
- Budget for dental, vision, and hearing coverage separately

Don't ignore this line item.

Sequence of Returns Risk

If you hit a market crash early in retirement, it can permanently damage your portfolio's longevity.

Strategies to mitigate:

- Have 1–3 years of expenses in cash or short-term bonds
- Use a flexible withdrawal rate (reduce spending in bad years)
- Create income floors (annuities, part-time work, pensions)
- Delay big discretionary spending until portfolio stabilizes

Your withdrawal strategy matters more than your exact number.

Turning Your FI Number Into a System

Once you know your FI number, build a system around it:

1. Automate investments to hit annual targets
2. Track expenses annually and compare to projection
3. Rebalance portfolio to stay on glide path
4. Use annual review to adjust for:

- Inflation
- Lifestyle changes
- Market performance
- Tax law changes

You're not guessing anymore. You're monitoring a model.

Engineer Scenarios

James, 33, Software Engineer

James calculated he needs $3.1M to support his desired $100K/year lifestyle. He's saving $48K/year and projects hitting FI by age 50. He plans to shift into semi-retirement (consulting 10 hrs/week) by 47.

Clara, 46, Mechanical Engineer

Clara uses a 3.25% withdrawal rate and has diversified across Roth, brokerage, and 457(b). Her $2.4M portfolio supports $78K/year with margin. She's running Monte Carlo simulations annually.

Raj, 55, Civil Engineer

Raj reached $2.8M in net worth, FI at age 54. He withdraws $95K/year but keeps $100K in cash as a buffer. His biggest concern is long-term healthcare.

Encouragement

You're more capable than you think.

Defining your FI number is one of the most powerful financial acts you can do. It transforms vague anxiety into measurable progress.

And once you define it, you can:

- Build toward it
- Adjust your career decisions around it
- Retire *to* something, not just *from* something

Financial independence isn't a fantasy.

It's a formula.

It's a system.

It's a strategy.

You just have to do the math.

Takeaways

- Your FI number = Annual spending ÷ safe withdrawal rate
- Adjust for inflation, taxes, healthcare, and sequence of returns risk
- Use future value projections and backtest different retirement paths
- Build a portfolio and withdrawal plan that's tax-efficient and resilient

The smartest engineers don't wait for retirement.

They define independence.

They engineer toward it.

They build lives on *their* terms.

Chapter 42: Building Wealth Using the FIRE Principles (Financial Independence, Retire Early)

There's a movement out there that has been quietly gaining momentum among high-income professionals, systems thinkers, and lifestyle renegades alike. It's called FIRE—Financial Independence, Retire Early. And it's about far more than sipping margaritas on a beach at age 35.

FIRE is about control.

It's about design.

It's about creating a life where your money works for you, not the other way around.

For engineers, it's also about systems thinking—modeling outcomes, optimizing inputs, reducing waste, and creating financial autonomy on your own terms.

In this chapter, we'll unpack how FIRE works, how to build toward it as an engineer, and how to decide whether full FIRE or some version of it is the right goal for you.

Because whether you're trying to escape the 9-to-5 or simply gain the freedom to pursue more meaningful work, the FIRE principles can serve as a framework for financial design that accelerates your goals and protects your options.

What Is FIRE?

FIRE stands for:

- **Financial Independence** – Having enough assets or income to cover your expenses without needing to work.
- **Retire Early** – Leaving traditional employment far earlier than the conventional retirement age.

But in practice, FIRE is flexible. There are variations:

- **LeanFIRE** – Retiring early with a modest lifestyle and very low expenses.
- **FatFIRE** – Retiring early with a higher standard of living and more financial cushion.
- **BaristaFIRE** – Reaching partial FI and working part-time or in passion projects.
- **CoastFIRE** – Saving aggressively early, then letting compound interest do the rest while you coast.

Why FIRE Resonates With Engineers

- You enjoy optimization.
- You're used to long-term modeling.
- You value autonomy.
- You understand the power of compounding.
- You may work in high-income roles and want to put that to use.

Most importantly, you want to design a system that frees your time.

The FIRE Formula – Core Concepts

FIRE can be broken into a simple, powerful formula:

1. **Know your annual spending**
2. **Multiply that by 25–33 (depending on your safe withdrawal rate)**
3. **That's your FI number**

Example:

- Annual spending: $70,000
- FI Number: $70,000 × 25 = $1.75 million (using 4%)

Save and invest until you reach that number, then design your exit.

But like any system, there's nuance and complexity under the hood.

Step 1: Track and Optimize Spending

Engineers often overlook this. They focus on income, not expenses.

But FIRE is built on your *spending.* The lower your spending:

- The less you need to save
- The faster you can reach FI
- The less you're dependent on market performance

Track every dollar for 3–6 months.

Segment expenses:

- Essentials: housing, food, insurance, healthcare
- Discretionary: entertainment, travel, restaurants
- Frictional waste: unused subscriptions, lifestyle creep, impulse purchases

Use tools:

- Personal Capital
- Mint
- YNAB (You Need A Budget)
- Excel or Google Sheets

Cutting spending is like reducing system load. It improves performance without increasing resource demand.

Step 2: Maximize Your Savings Rate

This is the single most predictive variable in FIRE math.

Traditional advice says save 10%–15%.

FIRE advice aims for 40%–70%.

Why?

Because savings rate dictates how many years you must work.

Sample table:

- Save 10% → FI in 51 years
- Save 30% → FI in 28 years
- Save 50% → FI in 17 years
- Save 70% → FI in 8.5 years

Engineers making $120K–$300K+ have the income to make this possible.

Ways to boost savings rate:

- House hack or live with roommates
- Drive older cars or use public transport
- Cook at home
- Max out 401(k), IRA, HSA
- Side hustle or freelance
- Live like a student even after promotions

FIRE isn't about deprivation. It's about alignment.

Step 3: Invest Aggressively and Intelligently

You can't save your way to FI. You must invest.

Strategies:

- Broad-based index funds (VTI, VTSAX, FZROX)
- Low-cost ETFs (S&P 500, total market, international)
- Maximize tax-advantaged accounts first
- Use taxable brokerage for overflow

Target asset allocation:

- 90% stocks / 10% bonds for aggressive FIRE

- Shift to 70/30 or 60/40 as you approach drawdown phase

Use dollar-cost averaging and automate investments.

Tools:

- Fidelity, Schwab, Vanguard
- M1 Finance (for easy rebalancing)
- Robo-advisors (Betterment, Wealthfront) if you want simplicity

Avoid high-fee funds, active trading, or stock picking unless you truly understand the risks.

Step 4: Increase Income

If cutting expenses is defense, increasing income is offense.

As an engineer, your earning potential is strong.

Ways to grow it:

- Ask for raises based on value created
- Job-hop strategically (engineering roles often offer 15–20% jumps)
- Earn certifications (PMP, PE, AWS, etc.)
- Freelance or consult on the side
- Build products or intellectual property
- Invest in real estate or content that earns passively

Step 5: Build Systems, Not Willpower

You're not trying to muscle through 10 years of deprivation.

You're designing:

- An automatic investment machine
- A budget that works without stress
- A workflow that prioritizes high-value tasks
- A lifestyle you enjoy now—not just someday

Examples:

- Pay yourself first (auto-transfer to investments on payday)
- Use calendar blocks for financial check-ins
- Create a "Spending Rules" doc to avoid emotional purchases

Think of FIRE as a set of control loops—not a set of sacrifices.

Step 6: Decide What Retirement Means to You

"Retire early" doesn't mean doing nothing. It means *choosing* what to do.

Options:

- Travel extensively
- Volunteer or mentor
- Start a business
- Teach or write
- Consult part-time
- Focus on family, hobbies, or health

Some FIRE engineers become full-time entrepreneurs. Others take sabbaticals. Others slow down and savor life.

The real win isn't early retirement—it's *agency.*

Engineer Scenarios

Natalie, 29, Software Engineer

Natalie saves 60% of her income, maxes out all retirement accounts, and keeps expenses under $40K. She's on track to reach FIRE by 38.

Marco, 41, Electrical Engineer

Marco discovered FIRE at 35. He increased his savings rate from 15% to 45%, paid off his house early, and now works 3 days/week by choice.

Erin, 37, Civil Engineer

Erin and her spouse reached CoastFIRE—enough invested to grow to full FI by 60 without saving another dime. Now they work in less stressful roles and enjoy more time with their kids.

Pros and Cons of the FIRE Path

Pros:

- Freedom of time and choice
- Flexibility in career decisions
- Reduced stress and burnout
- More intentional living
- Earlier pursuit of passion projects

Cons:

- Social pressure or judgment
- Requires discipline and delayed gratification
- Healthcare and insurance challenges pre-Medicare
- Sequence of returns risk in early retirement
- Potential under-spending or fear-based money habits

The FIRE movement is a tool—not a religion. Use what works. Discard what doesn't.

Action Steps for Engineers

1. Calculate your FIRE number (see Chapter 41)
2. Track your current savings rate
3. Audit your expenses for waste and misalignment
4. Maximize employer benefits (401(k) match, HSA, ESPP)
5. Automate monthly investments
6. Build 1–2 passive income streams
7. Create a written plan for what FIRE looks like for *you*

Encouragement

You're more capable than you think.

FIRE isn't about escaping life.

It's about *building* a life—on your terms, with your priorities, and without needing permission from a boss, a paycheck, or a quarterly review cycle.

It's about designing your future with intention.

Takeaways

- FIRE is a system of high savings, smart investing, and lifestyle design
- Engineers are uniquely suited for FIRE because of their analytical mindset and strong income potential
- The journey is flexible—FIRE has many flavors
- What matters most is clarity, structure, and sustainability

The smartest engineers don't just code systems—they *live* them.

They model outcomes.

They iterate designs.

They build lives worth living.

Chapter 43: Engineering a 10-Year Exit Plan

Every great design begins with a defined end state. In engineering, we reverse-engineer from that vision. We map the requirements, assess the risks, and create systems that can be tested, monitored, and optimized over time.

Financial independence works the same way.

This chapter is about building a 10-year exit plan—a personalized roadmap that lets you step away from full-time work on your terms. Whether that means retiring early, transitioning into consulting, starting a business, or working part-time doing something you love, the goal is the same: full control over your time and energy.

This plan isn't a fantasy.

It's a framework.

And you, as an engineer, are uniquely equipped to build it.

What Is a 10-Year Exit Plan?

A 10-year exit plan is a systematic strategy to reach financial independence (or a desired level of work-optional status) within a decade. It's a defined runway. A project plan. A financial design blueprint with milestones, constraints, variables, and stress tests.

It includes:

- Target net worth
- Ideal lifestyle and spending model

- Debt reduction or elimination timeline
- Asset accumulation strategy
- Income diversification
- Tax minimization framework
- Withdrawal sequencing logic

But most importantly, it includes your *why*—your definition of success, fulfillment, and freedom.

Why 10 Years?

Because 10 years is long enough to:

- Accumulate serious capital through compound growth
- Build habits that last
- Make mid-career transitions
- Course-correct without panic

And it's short enough to:

- Feel urgent
- Stay focused
- Avoid burnout from too long a grind

If you start now, 10 years from today can look radically different.

Step 1: Define Your Exit Vision

This is your "retirement spec sheet."

Answer:

- What will your lifestyle look like?
- Where will you live?
- How much will you spend?
- Will you still work part-time? Consult? Travel?
- What will your days *feel* like?

Quantify:

- Annual expenses in today's dollars
- Desired net worth
- Passive income needs

Example:

- Target spending: $90,000/year
- Withdrawal rate: 3.5%
- Needed portfolio: $2.57M

Add a buffer for:

- Market volatility
- Healthcare inflation
- Long-term care

Step 2: Take Inventory of Where You Are

Now build a baseline.

Document:

- Current income
- Savings rate
- Total net worth
- Asset allocation
- Account types (taxable, tax-deferred, tax-free)
- Monthly expenses
- Mortgage and debt balances

Example:

- Age: 38

- Net worth: $620,000
- Income: $165,000
- Savings rate: 28%
- Investments: 75/25 stock/bond

Step 3: Calculate the Gap

Use future value formulas to estimate where you'll be in 10 years *without* changes.

Then model where you *need* to be to hit your FI goal.

Gap = Target Net Worth - Projected Net Worth at Current Pace

Example:

- Projected in 10 years: $1.45M
- Target FI: $2.5M
- Gap: $1.05M

Now engineer a system to close that gap.

Step 4: Build Your Exit Timeline

Break the 10 years into clear phases:

Years 1–3: Foundation Building

- Max out tax-advantaged accounts
- Eliminate consumer debt
- Reduce lifestyle inflation
- Identify career upside (raises, promotions, job changes)

Years 4–7: Acceleration Phase

- Increase savings rate to 40% or more
- Add income streams (consulting, rentals, IP)
- Optimize asset location (taxable vs. Roth vs. traditional)
- Evaluate real estate or small business investments

Years 8–10: Stabilization & Preparation

- Pay off mortgage (optional)
- Shift allocation toward income/resilience assets
- Build 2–3 years of cash buffer
- Model withdrawal plans (Roth conversion ladders, SEPP, taxable bridges)

Step 5: Optimize the Levers

These are your variables to adjust over time:

Savings Rate

- Track monthly in % of gross and net income
- Automate increases after each raise

Spending Discipline

- Create caps on discretionary categories
- Reassess "wants" annually

Income Growth

- Change jobs if underpaid
- Monetize skills outside the 9-to-5

Investment Strategy

- Stick to index funds or a clear thesis
- Rebalance annually
- Avoid speculative distractions

Tax Strategy

- Harvest losses tactically
- Use HSAs for long-term health investing
- Consider backdoor Roth IRAs, mega backdoor Roths, and 457(b) accounts

Account Diversification

- Goal: 33% in taxable, 33% in Roth, 33% in traditional by retirement
- Allows for withdrawal flexibility and tax arbitrage

Step 6: Engineer an Exit Portfolio

As you approach year 10, reframe from accumulation to *preservation + cash flow.*

A typical exit portfolio might include:

- 60% total stock index
- 20% intermediate-term bonds
- 10% real estate (REITs or rentals)
- 5% cash equivalents (T-bills, high-yield savings)
- 5% alternatives or tilt (small-cap value, international, etc.)

Model:

- Sequence of returns risk
- 3.25% to 4.0% withdrawal rate simulations
- Asset depletion timelines

Step 7: Design Your Exit Trigger Conditions

Set specific financial and emotional benchmarks:

Hard Metrics:

- Portfolio value hits $2.5M
- Mortgage paid off or offset with passive cash flow

- 2 years of post-exit expenses in cash

Soft Metrics:

- Confidence in withdrawal strategy
- Meaningful use of time post-exit
- Partner/family support

Document this in a "Retirement Readiness Checklist."

Step 8: Prepare for Life After Exit

The goal isn't to escape work. It's to realign with purpose.

Consider:

- Identity and community post-career
- New routines and habits
- Projects or impact goals
- Health, fitness, and mental well-being

Use your engineering mindset to prototype a post-exit life:

- 30-day sabbatical test
- Part-time consulting pilot
- Volunteer or nonprofit immersion

Your 10-year exit isn't just about *leaving.* It's about *creating.*

Engineer Scenarios

Lucas, 42, Systems Engineer

Built a 10-year plan at 40. Increased his savings rate to 55%, acquired 3 rental properties, and is now 6 years from full FI. He plans to teach part-time.

Rachel, 35, Mechanical Engineer

Discovered FIRE late, but has been aggressively saving. With a $1.2M goal and a $200K annual savings plan, she's on track to exit by 45 with a portfolio of $2.4M.

Anand, 48, Electrical Engineer

Created an exit plan at 45. Included downsizing home, transitioning to remote consulting, and shifting to a 60/40 portfolio. Will reach work-optional status by 55.

Encouragement

You're more capable than you think.

A 10-year exit plan isn't a pipe dream.

It's a structured model.

It's a way to put engineering principles—feedback loops, scenario modeling, redundancy, stress-testing—to work in your financial life.

Build it with clarity.

Monitor it with discipline.

Adjust it with purpose.

Then walk away—when *you* decide—with confidence.

Takeaways

- Define your FI vision in concrete terms
- Calculate your net worth gap and reverse-engineer it
- Track savings, expenses, and investment growth in a structured plan
- Build buffers, diversify income, and optimize for taxes
- Create a checklist of both financial and emotional readiness

The smartest engineers don't just build bridges or code.

They build exits.

They design freedom.

They prototype their own autonomy.

Chapter 44: Early Retirement Pitfalls for Engineers

Retiring early might sound like the ultimate engineering problem solved: reduce expenses, maximize income, invest the surplus, hit your FIRE number, and flip the switch. In theory, it's a clean, elegant equation. But as every seasoned engineer knows, execution is where the real complexity shows up.

Early retirement—defined loosely as stepping away from full-time work before the traditional age of 60-65—requires not just mathematical preparation, but psychological readiness, systems design, contingency planning, and ongoing recalibration.

This chapter unpacks the most common and costly pitfalls engineers face when retiring early. It's not meant to scare you away from your goal. Quite the opposite. Think of this chapter like a stress test for your blueprint. If you address these pitfalls early, you engineer not just a retirement plan—but a resilient, adaptable, life-fulfilling exit strategy.

Pitfall #1: Underestimating Healthcare Costs

One of the biggest surprises early retirees face is the sheer cost and complexity of health insurance before Medicare eligibility kicks in at 65.

If you leave a W-2 job at 50 or 55, you need to budget for potentially 10-15 years of private insurance coverage. And those years can be costly.

Options include:

- ACA Marketplace Plans (with income-based subsidies if your taxable income is low)

- COBRA coverage from your last employer (usually 18 months max)
- Health Sharing Ministries (limited coverage and religious affiliation required)
- Part-time work with benefits
- Self-funded Health Reimbursement Arrangements (HRAs)

Action Steps:

- Build a line item for healthcare: assume $15,000/year for a couple
- Use Roth conversion planning and capital gains harvesting to keep income low
- Explore ACA subsidies carefully (a few thousand dollars of income can cost you $10,000+ in lost subsidies)
- Consider an HSA (Health Savings Account) as a long-term tax-advantaged savings tool

Pitfall #2: Overestimating Withdrawal Rates

The classic 4% rule is a helpful starting point, but it's not a guarantee. Especially if you plan to retire before 60.

Why?

- Longer retirement periods increase risk of outliving money
- Sequence of returns risk is amplified
- Inflation may be higher than expected
- Expenses often increase, not decrease

What engineers often miss:

- The 4% rule is based on a 30-year retirement horizon
- If you're retiring at 45, you might need that money to last 40+ years
- 3.25% or even 3.0% may be more realistic

Action Steps:

- Use dynamic models, not static rules of thumb
- Build contingency plans: spending adjustments, part-time work, rental income
- Create multiple buckets: short-term cash, medium-term bonds, long-term equities

Pitfall #3: Forgetting About Taxes in Retirement

Many early retirees assume their tax burden will go down when they stop working. But that's not always true.

Why?

- Traditional 401(k)/IRA withdrawals are taxed as ordinary income
- Capital gains from selling appreciated assets can push you into higher brackets
- Medicare premiums (IRMAA) are income-based and can increase costs dramatically
- State taxes may still apply even without earned income

Engineers especially face complexity if they:

- Have significant RSU or ESPP holdings
- Receive deferred compensation
- Own rental real estate
- Want to do Roth conversions during low-income years

Action Steps:

- Create a "retirement tax map" showing each account type and its tax treatment
- Optimize your tax brackets by sequencing withdrawals
- Consider moving to a tax-friendly state

- Use a CPA who specializes in retirement and early withdrawal strategies

Pitfall #4: Retiring to Nothing

Early retirement isn't a solution to burnout. It's an empty container. And if you don't fill it intentionally, it can lead to:

- Boredom
- Loss of identity
- Marital stress
- Anxiety or depression

Engineers are especially vulnerable here because so much of your identity may be tied to your technical competence, your team, your projects, your reputation.

When that structure disappears, some feel unmoored.

Action Steps:

- Design your *ideal week* before you leave work
- Test the lifestyle with mini-sabbaticals or part-time transitions
- Find new structures: volunteering, mentoring, writing, traveling, building something else
- Consider the psychological concept of FIRE: not Financial Independence Retire Early, but *Freedom, Identity, Routine, Engagement*

Pitfall #5: Sequence of Returns Risk

This risk isn't just academic. It's a real killer of retirement plans.

It means that *when* you get bad market returns matters just as much as *if* you get them.

If you retire and withdraw money during a downturn in the first 5 years, it can permanently damage your portfolio.

Action Steps:

- Maintain a cash buffer of 1-3 years of expenses
- Use a flexible withdrawal strategy: cut back in bad years
- Consider guardrails: start at 3.25%, but increase or decrease based on performance
- Use annuities *selectively* to create a base level of income

Pitfall #6: Ignoring Longevity Risk

You might live longer than you think.

Engineering brains like to use averages:

- Life expectancy = 78 (men), 82 (women)

But averages are not guarantees. You might live to 90, 95, or beyond. That's 40+ years of self-funded living if you retire at 55.

Action Steps:

- Plan for at least 35 years of retirement
- Maintain some equity exposure even in later decades
- Build income streams that are inflation-adjusted
- Consider long-term care planning

Pitfall #7: Not Stress Testing the Plan

Engineers test everything before deployment. So test your retirement plan.

Stress test:

- Bear markets in the first 3 years
- Healthcare shock
- $5,000/month lifestyle instead of $4,000
- College costs for kids
- Divorce or caregiving for aging parents

Tools to use:

- FIRECalc
- Portfolio Visualizer
- Pralana Gold or NewRetirement calculators
- Monte Carlo simulations with conservative assumptions

Pitfall #8: Underestimating Inflation

Most engineers account for 2% or 2.5% inflation in their models. But what if it runs hotter for longer?

Action Steps:

- Use 3% or 3.5% in your baseline model
- Include inflation hedges: TIPS, I Bonds, REITs, dividend growth stocks
- Model different inflation scenarios and withdrawal stress points

Pitfall #9: Believing Early Retirement Is the End Goal

It's not. It's the *starting point.*

Early retirement is a bridge—not a destination. It frees your time, but that time must be invested wisely.

Ask yourself:

- What do I want more time *for*?
- What unfinished projects or dreams will I pursue?
- How will I stay mentally sharp, socially engaged, and physically active?

Your engineering brain craves complexity and mastery. Make sure your retirement plan includes space for both.

Real-World Example: Olivia, Software Engineer, Retired at 45

- Saved $2.2M
- Assumed $80,000/year expenses
- Retired in 2021—then hit the 2022 downturn
- Adjusted withdrawals down to 3.25%, picked up a part-time teaching gig

- Says: "The plan wasn't wrong, but the flexibility was key."

Real-World Example: Dan, Mechanical Engineer, Retired at 50

- Net worth: $2.7M
- Unexpected costs: healthcare rose 22%, daughter moved back home
- Started consulting part-time again, not for the money but for identity and routine

Encouragement

You're more capable than you think.

You can design a resilient early retirement plan.

You can navigate uncertainty, market noise, and emotional complexity.

You can iterate your way forward.

But you must plan *beyond* the math.

Takeaways

- Early retirement isn't just a financial challenge—it's a life systems challenge
- Model your plan with conservative assumptions and aggressive contingencies
- Plan for taxes, healthcare, and identity *before* you retire
- Test your portfolio, your withdrawal plan, and your lifestyle before you leap
- Focus less on "retiring early" and more on "living deliberately"

The smartest engineers don't just automate the future.

They simulate it.

They model stress.

They optimize for failure.

And that's how they build systems that endure.

Chapter 45: Lifestyle Design: Building a Life Beyond Your Work Identity

For many engineers, work isn't just what you do.

It's who you are.

From the first day of undergrad or the first software bootcamp, your brain has been wired to solve, optimize, design, troubleshoot. You took pride in being the one who made systems work. You worked long hours not just for the paycheck, but for the dopamine hit of building something elegant, effective, and scalable.

That identity often compounds over decades: "I'm a civil engineer." "I'm a product architect." "I'm a problem solver."

But what happens when you step away from the job—by choice, burnout, layoff, or early retirement?

Who are you without the title?

What gives your life structure without the stand-ups, code reviews, or client walkthroughs?

This chapter is about designing a lifestyle that doesn't just *replace* your work identity—it *expands* your sense of self.

It's about shifting from defining yourself by what you produce, to how you live.

From building systems at work, to building a life of purpose, curiosity, joy, and contribution.

And if you approach it like an engineer, lifestyle design can be the most meaningful project you'll ever take on.

The Problem with Identity Tied to Work

Let's start with an uncomfortable truth: if you've been praised, rewarded, and relied upon for your technical skills for decades, it's likely your self-worth is tied to your job.

Signs:

- You feel anxious when asked "So what do you do?"
- You work late even when it's not necessary
- You check Slack or email on vacation
- You struggle to enjoy downtime
- You fear retirement not because of money, but because of boredom

This identity fusion is normal. But it's not sustainable.

You are more than your job description.

Lifestyle Design Defined

Lifestyle design means intentionally crafting the structure, activities, and values of your life *outside* of work.

It means reverse-engineering your days, weeks, and years to align with what truly matters.

It includes:

- How you spend your time
- Who you spend it with
- What projects you engage in
- Where you live
- What routines energize you
- How you maintain health, connection, and curiosity

You become the lead architect of your own experience.

Principle #1: Design Around Values, Not Just Goals

Most engineers love goals. Numbers. Deadlines.

"Run a marathon."

"Build a passive income stream."

"Travel to 12 countries."

But goals without values are hollow.

Design around your core values:

- Autonomy
- Adventure
- Contribution
- Learning
- Family
- Health
- Creativity

Ask: What kind of *life* am I trying to live?

Then align your calendar with those answers.

Example: If you value creativity, carve out 10 hours/week for building, writing, painting, or designing—even if there's no monetary ROI.

Principle #2: Prototype Your Lifestyle Like a Product

Don't wait until retirement to test your dream life. Prototype it.

Run sprints:

- Take a 1-month mini-sabbatical
- Try working 4 days/week
- Spend a summer living in a different city
- Go one month without checking email after 5 p.m.

Just like with engineering projects, you don't guess your way to a successful product. You build MVPs. You iterate.

Do the same with your lifestyle.

Principle #3: Build a Daily Structure That Serves You

Without a job, your calendar is a blank slate. That can be liberating—or disorienting.

Engineers thrive on systems. So build one:

- Morning rituals (e.g., workout, journaling, reading)
- Theme days (e.g., Mondays = writing, Wednesdays = volunteering)
- Scheduled time blocks (e.g., 9-12 = focused project, 2-3 = learning)
- Regular review sessions (e.g., Sunday night planning)

Freedom without structure is chaos.

Freedom *with* structure is power.

Principle #4: Diversify Your Identity

Think of identity like an investment portfolio.

If 100% of your identity is tied up in being an engineer, you're vulnerable.

Instead, diversify into:

- Family roles (partner, parent, sibling)
- Creative outlets (writer, musician, tinkerer)
- Social roles (mentor, volunteer, neighbor)
- Physical pursuits (hiker, dancer, lifter)
- Intellectual identities (reader, thinker, learner)

You become more resilient when one role shifts or disappears.

Principle #5: Curate Relationships Intentionally

Your coworkers may have been your social circle. When you leave, there can be a vacuum.

Fill it deliberately:

- Join local clubs or mastermind groups
- Volunteer in causes that matter to you
- Reconnect with old friends
- Schedule recurring activities (hiking groups, book clubs, game nights)

Loneliness is one of the most under-discussed risks of early retirement.

Connection doesn't happen by accident. Design it.

Principle #6: Keep Building

You don't need to build for a paycheck.

Build for joy.

Build for impact.

Build because it's who you are.

Engineers don't stop being engineers.

You just shift what you engineer:

- Build a garden
- Build a community tool library
- Build a course to teach young students
- Build a tiny home, a podcast, or a mentorship platform

Your skills don't expire when you retire.

Your value doesn't either.

Real-Life Example: Tim, 48, Electrical Engineer

Tim hit his FIRE number and retired at 47. At first, he loved the freedom. But 6 months in, he felt restless. He missed solving problems.

So he started tutoring high school students in physics. He joined a nonprofit that builds solar panels for off-grid schools. Now he says:

"I don't feel like I retired. I just stopped reporting to someone else."

Real-Life Example: Anita, 53, Software Architect

Anita designed her ideal week before quitting. Monday and Tuesday mornings = project time. Wednesday = hiking. Friday = date day with her spouse.

"I realized that without a plan, I'd just scroll my way through retirement. Now I have a life I don't want to retire *from*."

Action Steps

1. List your top 5 values
2. Sketch your ideal day, week, and year
3. Run a 30-day lifestyle sprint (test a new routine)
4. Identify roles you want to expand beyond "engineer"
5. Block time each week for play, service, movement, connection, and creativity

Encouragement

You're more capable than you think.

Your life is bigger than your job.

Your worth isn't in your output.

Your joy doesn't need permission.

Design it.

Test it.

Iterate it.

Live it.

Takeaways

- Work identity is powerful, but not permanent
- Lifestyle design is an ongoing process, not a one-time plan
- Engineers thrive when they apply design thinking to their own lives
- Structure, values, community, and purpose are key to thriving post-career

The smartest engineers don't just build code or bridges.

They build lives worth living.

They build routines that energize.

They build futures with freedom.

You don't have to retire *from* something.

You can retire *into* something.

Part X: Teaching, Legacy, and Life After Work

In Part X, we shift from accumulation to significance. This section is about what comes *after* wealth building, after spreadsheets, after early retirement models and tax optimization. It's about meaning. It's about passing on more than money. For engineers, who've spent a career building systems, solving problems, and refining processes, legacy planning is the final—and perhaps most important—design challenge.

We'll explore how to teach financial literacy to your kids, mentees, or community. We'll unpack how to document your wisdom and engineer generational systems of support. You'll learn how to transition from achiever to advisor, from practitioner to teacher, from builder to mentor. We'll also address how to think about charitable giving, philanthropic projects, and creating an enduring impact that reflects your values.

The goal isn't just to retire. It's to inspire. It's to build something that lasts beyond your job title. And it's to recognize that your greatest contribution might not be what you did for work—but how you helped others find their path.

Chapter 46: Philanthropy and Giving Back as an Engineer

Let's get one thing clear right away: giving back doesn't require you to be a millionaire. It doesn't require a foundation or a family name chiseled into a hospital wing. What it does require is a shift in mindset: from accumulation to impact, from optimization to contribution, from me to we.

As an engineer, you are uniquely wired to make meaningful contributions. You think in systems. You plan with precision. You analyze outcomes. Philanthropy—done intentionally—can become one of the most powerful and rewarding applications of your skill set. Not as a side project, but as a core piece of your financial life plan.

This chapter is about integrating giving into your wealth strategy. It's about purposefully engineering generosity.

Why Giving Matters

Most people think giving is about the recipient. But seasoned givers know: it transforms the giver too.

Giving re-centers your values. It reminds you that wealth is a tool, not the end goal. It reinforces your agency and legacy. And perhaps most important, it counterbalances the often narrow, numbers-focused mindset that dominates financial thinking.

Engineers benefit from that recalibration. Because the danger isn't that you won't be successful. The danger is that you'll hit all your financial goals—and still feel like something is missing.

Defining Your Giving Philosophy

Just like with investment strategies, giving should be guided by a clear philosophy.

Ask yourself:

- What causes make me angry, hopeful, or energized?
- What communities or problems do I care most about?
- What kind of change do I want to help bring about—in the next 5 years or 50?
- Do I want to be involved hands-on, or simply support existing work?
- What does "enough" look like for me personally, so I can give the rest freely?

Once you answer those questions, your giving strategy becomes far more focused and joyful.

Types of Giving Engineers Often Overlook

1. **Time-Based Giving**

- Mentoring young engineers
- Volunteering to teach coding or robotics
- Serving on nonprofit boards
- Offering pro-bono consulting for infrastructure or IT projects

1. **Skills-Based Giving**

- Helping nonprofits improve data systems
- Building low-cost prototypes for clean water, renewable energy, or education
- Designing software or automation tools for under-resourced causes

1. **Money-Based Giving**

- Donor-Advised Funds (DAFs)
- Recurring monthly donations
- One-time legacy gifts in your will
- Endowed scholarships for future engineers

How to Budget for Giving

The easiest way to start giving is to make it a line item. If you wait until you "feel rich enough," you'll keep kicking the can down the road.

Engineers often appreciate formulas:

- 1% of your income to causes that matter
- 5% after you hit your emergency fund and retirement savings goals
- 10% when you're financially independent

You can also tie giving to milestones:

- Bonus at work = 10% to charity
- Investment gain = tithe a portion
- New job or exit = create a giving fund

Start small. Stay consistent. Scale when you're ready.

Donor-Advised Funds: A Powerful Giving Vehicle

If you want to give strategically but not all at once, a DAF is a smart move.

It works like this:

1. You donate assets (cash, stocks, etc.) to the DAF and get a tax deduction that year.
2. The money grows tax-free in the DAF.
3. You recommend grants to charities over time.

Pros:

- Immediate tax deduction

- Investment growth
- No pressure to give all at once
- Keeps your giving organized

Cons:

- Irrevocable once donated
- Small administrative fees
- Requires due diligence to vet charities

For engineers who like systems and flexibility, DAFs are a perfect fit.

Real-World Example: Sam, 42, Data Engineer

Sam and his partner decided to give 1% of their annual income to support STEM access in rural schools. They started a donor-advised fund, set up monthly contributions, and visited one of the robotics programs they helped fund. Sam said, "It was like seeing a mirror of myself as a kid—but with fewer resources. We didn't just write a check. We rewrote the equation."

Tax-Optimized Giving

Giving can also reduce your tax bill. Here are a few ways:

- **Donate appreciated stock**: Avoid capital gains and get a full deduction.
- **Qualified Charitable Distributions (QCDs)**: Once you're 70½, you can give directly from your IRA.
- **Bunching**: Combine two years of donations into one year to itemize deductions.
- **Giving during high-income years**: Offset tax liability while you're earning the most.

Speak with a CPA or advisor to align giving with your overall tax strategy.

Teaching Through Giving

Want your kids or mentees to be generous? Show them.

- Involve them in selecting causes.
- Let them "pitch" a charity and donate together.
- Create a family giving night.
- Share why you give, not just that you give.

Generosity is contagious. But it needs to be modeled.

Legacy Giving

If you want your giving to outlast you, build it into your estate plan.

Options include:

- Charitable bequests in your will
- Naming a charity as a beneficiary on a retirement account
- Creating a charitable trust
- Establishing an endowed scholarship or fund

Ask:

- What story do I want my money to tell after I'm gone?
- How can my engineering career fund the next generation of change-makers?

Giving Without Regret

Some engineers are reluctant to give because they fear mismanagement or inefficiency. That's valid. But don't let perfect be the enemy of good.

Strategies:

- Use Charity Navigator or GuideStar to vet organizations
- Start local and build relationships with organizations
- Focus on causes with measurable impact
- Set limits: "I give $5,000/year and revisit every January."

You can always adjust. But waiting for certainty means waiting forever.

Giving as Part of Your Identity

Ultimately, giving is less about money than about meaning.

You don't have to be a billionaire philanthropist. You just have to be willing to share what you have, when you can, with intention.

Engineers often retire with more than enough.

But giving isn't the result of abundance.

It's the source of it.

Encouragement

You're more capable than you think.

Your wealth can do more than fund your lifestyle.

It can shape lives, spark possibility, and outlive you.

You know how to build systems. Now you can build legacies.

Takeaways

- Philanthropy is a tool for purpose, not just a tax write-off
- Start with values, not just donations
- Use DAFs, stock donations, and QCDs to maximize impact
- Involve family and mentees to build a culture of generosity
- Engineer your giving like your portfolio: strategically, intentionally, and consistently

The smartest engineers don't just optimize wealth.

They redirect it.

They redesign impact.

They rebuild the world they want to live in.

Chapter 47: Teaching Financial Literacy to Your Family and Community

As engineers, you're trained to break down complex systems into understandable parts. That same mindset makes you perfectly suited to teach one of the most important systems anyone will ever interact with: money.

Financial literacy isn't about knowing everything. It's about having the confidence to ask questions, spot patterns, and make thoughtful decisions. This chapter is your blueprint for passing that mindset on—to your kids, your spouse, your extended family, and even your community.

Because if we're honest, it doesn't matter how well you manage your own portfolio if the people you love are drowning in debt, living paycheck to paycheck, or terrified of retirement.

Teaching isn't an add-on.

It's part of your legacy.

Where to Start: The Mindset Shift

Before you teach budgeting or compound interest, start with mindset.

Money is emotional. It's tied to self-worth, stress, opportunity, shame, and power. Help your loved ones understand that financial literacy isn't about being perfect. It's about being curious, consistent, and proactive.

Remind them:

- Everyone starts somewhere.
- You don't have to know everything to start making better decisions.

- Financial mistakes are lessons, not indictments.
- Talking about money isn't taboo—it's a tool for growth.

Start With the Basics

Here's a curriculum you can adapt depending on age and life stage:

For Kids (Ages 5-12)

- What is money? (trade, value, work)
- Needs vs. wants
- Earning through chores
- Saving in a jar or envelope
- Giving to others (start small: birthdays, holidays)

For Teens (Ages 13-18)

- Budgeting their allowance or part-time income
- Understanding credit and debit
- Compound interest and why early saving matters
- Basics of investing (index funds, not stock tips)
- Avoiding lifestyle creep

For Young Adults (Ages 18-25)

- Credit scores and reports
- Student loans: repayment strategies
- Taxes: why withholding matters
- Retirement accounts (401(k), Roth IRA)
- Rent vs. buy, emergency funds

For Adults (25+)

- Investment allocation basics
- Insurance 101

- How to spot a financial scam
- Planning for kids' college or a second home
- Estate planning: wills, trusts, beneficiaries

Each of these topics can be turned into a short conversation, a dinner table game, or a worksheet. You don't need to give a lecture—just guide the discussion.

Tools You Can Use

- Share your favorite books, YouTube channels, or podcasts
- Use spreadsheet templates to build mock budgets
- Track your own net worth and explain what it means
- Watch videos about credit, taxes, or investing together
- Open an investment account with your teen and let them research funds

Engineer the Habit

Repetition matters more than perfection.

Set a recurring time to talk about money. It could be:

- First Sunday of every month (Money Sunday)
- During road trips
- When preparing taxes
- After a big purchase or windfall

Ask questions like:

- What do you want money to help you do?
- What was the best/worst purchase you made this month?
- If you had $10,000 to invest, what would you do?
- What did you learn about money this year?

These conversations normalize money talk and create an open environment where no one feels judged.

Teaching Your Spouse or Partner

This is where many engineers struggle. You may be the spreadsheet-wielding optimizer, and your spouse may be more values-based or intuitive. That's okay.

Tips:

- Focus on shared goals (vacations, retirement, stability)
- Schedule money meetings with snacks, not stress
- Let each person have a "no-questions-asked" spending bucket
- Keep financial dashboards visual and simple
- Don't condescend; collaborate

Remember: Harmony > efficiency. The best financial plan is one you can both live with.

Teaching Extended Family (Without Being Preachy)

Sometimes you're the first in your family to "get it" financially. That comes with responsibility—and temptation. Don't become the know-it-all. Be the coach, not the critic.

Ideas:

- Share your favorite money podcast or video after watching it yourself
- Offer to help build a budget template or plan for a goal
- Host a casual family workshop during the holidays
- Share your own mistakes and what you learned
- Offer to help with a credit repair or debt payoff strategy

Lead with empathy. Most financial problems stem from lack of access to information or emotional money habits inherited over time.

Teaching in Your Community

You don't need to be a certified financial planner to teach financial literacy at your kid's school, local library, church, or engineering meetup.

Ideas:

- Start a Financial Literacy Night for teens
- Offer a workshop on student loans or salary negotiation
- Partner with a nonprofit or STEM club
- Share your journey from broke grad student to financially confident engineer

Teaching isn't just about facts. It's about modeling calm, rational, values-aligned financial thinking in a world flooded with hype.

Real-World Story: Maya, Civil Engineer

Maya started teaching her two kids about money by giving them three jars: Spend, Save, and Give. She opened a 529 college plan and showed them the balance monthly. Now in high school, her son invests part of his summer job paycheck in a Roth IRA. Maya says, "He's seen the graph. He's seen the power of time. I didn't lecture. I just kept showing up."

When They Don't Listen

Sometimes the people you love don't want your advice. Let go of control. Be patient.

Instead:

- Be consistent, not controlling
- Share stories instead of lectures
- Celebrate small wins with them
- Keep modeling good behavior
- Invite them into decisions ("Want to help me pick our vacation savings goal?")

Change often happens slowly—then all at once.

Building a Financial Literacy Culture

If you want to change generational wealth in your family or community, you need a culture shift:

- Normalize talking about salaries
- Celebrate debt freedom like graduations

- Treat wealth-building as a team sport
- Make money values part of your family identity
- Leave behind shame and replace it with structure

Encouragement

You're more capable than you think.

You already teach others how to solve problems. Now you're helping them solve the one that matters most: financial stress.

Takeaways

- Start small: teach one person, one principle, this month
- Use your engineering mindset to simplify complex ideas
- Build money conversations into your routines
- Focus on mindset, not just mechanics
- Lead with love, not judgment

The smartest engineers don't just build wealth. They build financial systems that others can learn from, grow through, and eventually pass on.

You're not just teaching money.

You're teaching freedom.

You're teaching power.

You're teaching future engineers to think bigger than just their careers.

Chapter 48: Transition Planning: Retirement Isn't Just About Money

Retirement is the financial finish line that most engineers obsess over. But what happens when you cross that line?

The truth is, planning for retirement is about more than hitting your savings target. It's about identity, purpose, routine, health, and legacy. If you think retirement is just a math problem, you're going to have a hard time solving for happiness once work is over.

This chapter explores the hidden emotional and structural transitions that come with retirement—and how to prepare like an engineer.

Retirement Is a System, Not an Event

You're used to designing systems that are resilient, efficient, and durable. Retirement should be no different.

Your retirement isn't a single decision; it's a phased system:

- Pre-retirement (10-5 years out): Visioning and financial modeling
- Early retirement (first 5 years): Adjustment, exploration
- Mid-retirement (5-15 years in): Settling into identity
- Late retirement (15+ years): Health, legacy, caretaking

Each phase requires more than asset allocation. It demands a new way of thinking.

Step 1: Define Your Purpose Post-Paycheck

Many engineers go from being respected, busy professionals to retirees with too much time and too little direction.

Questions to ask:

- What do you want your days to look like?
- What problems will you still solve?
- What relationships need nurturing?
- What do you want to give back?
- What would excite you to wake up for?

Create a list of activities that stimulate your mind, keep your body active, and feed your soul. From teaching STEM classes to building furniture to mentoring startups—your next chapter should feel aligned, not aimless.

Step 2: Simulate the Schedule Before You Commit

Before you pull the retirement trigger, test-drive the lifestyle.

- Take a sabbatical or extended vacation
- Try living on your projected retirement budget
- Volunteer for a cause you care about
- Create a "retirement week" schedule and live it for 30 days

This helps reveal:

- Gaps in your social calendar
- Unrealistic budget expectations
- Hidden mental health triggers (like isolation or boredom)

Step 3: Budget for Lifestyle, Not Just Survival

Most retirement calculators assume a decrease in spending. That may not be true if:

- You want to travel extensively
- You want to help fund grandkids' education
- You want to support causes

- You're pursuing new hobbies (golf, classic car restoration, etc.)

Use three models:

- Bare minimum (roof, food, health)
- Comfortable (routine leisure, some travel)
- Ideal (dream lifestyle, bucket list goals)

Plan for flexibility between the three. Life evolves.

Step 4: Account for Non-Financial Risks

Money isn't the only factor in successful retirement.

- Health changes (mobility, chronic illness)
- Spousal differences (one retired, one not)
- Loss of social networks
- Identity shifts (from engineer to…?)
- Cognitive decline

Prepare like an engineer:

- Model your healthcare trajectory
- Create social routines
- Build a new identity blueprint

Step 5: Redesign Your Decision-Making System

During your working years, decisions were filtered through career consequences. Now you need new criteria:

- Does this align with my values?
- Is this activity energizing or draining?
- Does it protect or promote my health?
- Will this create memories or meaning?

Instead of optimizing for return on investment (ROI), you're optimizing for joy, energy, and legacy.

Step 6: Rebuild Relationships

Work often structures our social life. Without it, relationships need intentional care.

Strategies:

- Reconnect with old friends (schedule calls or visits)
- Join clubs, groups, or volunteer orgs
- Attend reunions, conferences, alumni events
- Deepen relationships with spouse and family

If your spouse retires at a different time than you, discuss expectations early. Household roles shift. Space and time expectations must be renegotiated.

Step 7: Create Your Legacy System

Retirement is a chance to plant seeds that outlive you.

- Document your knowledge (write, record, publish)
- Teach what you know (community colleges, high schools, online)
- Mentor young engineers
- Contribute to causes aligned with your values
- Develop family traditions, giving practices, or financial guidance for heirs

Legacy isn't just what you leave behind. It's what you live now.

Step 8: Engineer a New Identity

Who are you when you're no longer "the engineer at XYZ Corp"?

Retirement is a transition from doing to being.

You are not your W-2.

You are not your last title.

You are not your earnings report.

Try these prompts:

- I feel most like myself when I...
- I want to be remembered as someone who...
- I now have time to finally...

Your new identity can include:

- Author
- Volunteer
- Investor
- Coach
- Grandparent
- Creator
- Explorer
- Builder

Step 9: Create a Dashboard for Retirement Metrics

Engineers like to track.

Create a retirement dashboard that includes:

- Net worth
- Monthly cash flow
- Time allocation (how are you spending hours?)
- Bucket list items completed
- Health metrics (steps, weight, checkups)
- Relationships nurtured (calls, visits)

Track what matters to YOU. This is your system now.

Step 10: Know That It Will Evolve

Most retirees pivot 2-3 times in their first 10 years. The dream vacation lifestyle gets old. Health demands change. You miss solving hard problems.

Expect evolution. Design for iteration.

This is your encore—not your exit.

You still get to:

- Solve real problems
- Design solutions
- Optimize systems
- Teach, influence, guide

But now you do it on your terms.

Encouragement

You're more capable than you think.

Retirement isn't the end of engineering.

It's just a chance to engineer a better, freer, more meaningful life—with purpose, flexibility, and joy as your new KPIs.

Takeaways

- Start transition planning at least 5 years before your target date
- Focus on relationships, identity, and purpose as much as savings
- Create routines, roles, and rhythms before Day 1 of retirement
- Design your retirement as a phased system, not a single event
- Review and adjust every 6-12 months like you would any other system

Prompt to Reflect

What system can you start building now that will give your post-retirement life structure, energy, and meaning?

Retirement isn't just about money.

It's about freedom.

And freedom without purpose is just disconnection.

Engineer it better.

Design it smarter.

Live it fully.

Chapter 49: Continuous Improvement: Your Financial Kaizen

When engineers hear the word "Kaizen," it probably brings to mind the legendary Japanese principles of lean manufacturing, Toyota production systems, or Six Sigma quality management. Kaizen, at its core, means continuous improvement. It's the practice of making small, incremental enhancements over time, leading to massive long-term transformation. It is the engineering equivalent of steady iteration: the prototype becomes a product, the product becomes a system, the system becomes a legacy.

What if you applied Kaizen to your money?

This chapter is about taking your engineering mindset—the systems thinking, data-driven analysis, and long-term optimization—and applying it to your financial life in a way that's not just strategic, but sustainable. This is not about a one-time budgeting overhaul. This is about embracing improvement as a habit. A mindset. A way of life.

Let's walk through what Financial Kaizen looks like for engineers at every stage.

Financial Kaizen Begins with a System

The first rule of Financial Kaizen is that you need a repeatable system. Not a mood. Not a New Year's resolution. A system. Engineers know that if it can't be measured, it can't be managed. So your first move is creating a repeatable rhythm that lets you monitor, analyze, and adjust:

- Monthly money review: Where did your money go? Was that aligned with your goals?
- Quarterly strategy tune-up: Are you still tracking toward your FIRE number, early retirement goal, or real estate expansion?
- Annual comprehensive review: Did you improve from last year? How did your net worth, investment returns, and savings rate change?

The Feedback Loop: Your Personal PDCA Cycle

Engineers often use the Plan-Do-Check-Act (PDCA) cycle for continuous improvement. Let's reframe that for personal finance:

Plan – Define goals, project future income and expenses, map out tax strategy, estimate your retirement number.

Do – Automate investments, follow your savings allocation, implement new insurance policies, negotiate raises or side income.

Check – Track performance, measure ROI, analyze spending, compare actual vs. projected cash flow.

Act – Adjust savings rate, rebalance portfolio, shift tax strategy, reallocate time or money based on new priorities.

And then… start again.

Financial Engineering: Building, Stress Testing, and Optimizing

As engineers, you already understand how to analyze problems, anticipate variables, and test for edge cases. Apply that logic to your financial planning:

- Build a financial prototype: Use a spreadsheet to simulate your budget, savings rate, and projected net worth over time.
- Stress test your income: What happens if you lose your job? Can your emergency fund handle it?
- Stress test your investments: What if the market drops 30%? Do you have the time horizon and asset mix to withstand it?
- Stress test your life: What if you have a child? Lose a spouse? Start a business? What's the impact?

Financial Kaizen means preparing for what you *can't* control by optimizing what you *can.*

Micro-Iterations: The Hidden Power of 1% Improvements

Kaizen is about improvement by inches, not leaps. It's about getting 1% better—every day, every decision. That could look like:

- Increasing your 401(k) contribution by 1% each quarter
- Lowering your fixed expenses by $25/month by cutting unused subscriptions
- Negotiating one bill per year (insurance, cell phone, internet)
- Learning one new financial concept every week (read one chapter, listen to one podcast, talk to one expert)

Small hinges swing big doors. And when you compound dozens of tiny tweaks across decades? That's how you engineer wealth.

Financial Experiments: Data > Emotion

A core tenet of engineering is experimentation. In finance, that means trying new tactics—but tracking the results like a lab test:

- Try automating your savings through a "pay yourself first" system. Did it improve consistency?
- Experiment with different asset allocations and use back-testing tools. What mix suits your risk tolerance?
- Pilot a side hustle. What's the ROI on your time?
- Use cash envelopes for discretionary spending one month. Did you spend less?

Document, review, and adapt. Don't guess. Measure.

Modeling the Future: Using Tools to Simulate Outcomes

Financial software like Excel, Tiller, Personal Capital, or DIY spreadsheets can help you simulate outcomes based on different decisions:

- What happens if you retire at 55 vs 65?

- What if your investment returns are 5% vs. 7%?
- How does a real estate portfolio perform vs. index funds over 30 years?
- What's the tax impact of converting a traditional IRA to a Roth IRA in early retirement?

Don't just pick a path. Model the variables. That's what engineers do best.

Build a Financial Dashboard (and Actually Use It)

What gets monitored gets improved. Engineers use dashboards for performance. You can too:

- Net worth tracker
- Monthly cash flow report
- FIRE number progress
- Investment performance
- Insurance coverage checklist
- Tax planning worksheet

Check it monthly. Update it quarterly. Review it annually. That's your control panel.

Kaizen as a Culture: Bring Your Family Along

The best systems don't stop with you. Invite your spouse, kids, or community into the mindset:

- Hold quarterly family money meetings
- Teach your kids the budgeting app you use
- Share your spreadsheet with your spouse
- Start a financial book club with coworkers

Kaizen is contagious. So model the behavior and share the system.

When Life Changes, So Should the System

Your Kaizen system isn't static. Just like an engineer would update schematics after a design change, you should:

- Adjust savings after a raise
- Re-run simulations after a new child, house, or job
- Reevaluate insurance after milestones
- Refactor your portfolio annually

You don't need a full overhaul. Just keep iterating.

The Mindset Shift: From Reactive to Proactive

Engineers are builders by nature. But too many treat their money passively. Financial Kaizen flips that:

- You go from guessing to modeling
- From reacting to initiating
- From scattered to structured
- From unsure to iterative

You stop waiting for perfect and start improving consistently.

Final Thought

If you've made it this far in the book, you've already proven one thing:

You care.

Now it's time to systematize that care. To stop relying on bursts of motivation and start relying on structure. To stop waiting for perfect conditions and start improving today.

You don't need a finance degree. You don't need a six-figure salary. You just need a mindset—a Kaizen approach—to get 1% better every day.

Because the smartest engineers don't guess with money.

They model it. Monitor it. Improve it.

And then they go live the life they designed—by choice, not by chance.

You're more capable than you think.

Start improving. Start today.

Chapter 50: Final Words: Engineering a Life of Wealth, Purpose, and Freedom

You've come a long way.

If you've made it to Chapter 50, it means you've spent serious time thinking about your money, your future, your responsibilities, your dreams. And it also means you've done something that too few people do—you've taken ownership of your financial life. That alone is something to celebrate.

But this chapter isn't just a summary. It's a call to action.

It's the point in the blueprint where you step back from the detailed schematics and ask, "What am I really building?" Because in the end, wealth alone isn't the goal. Wealth is a tool. A powerful one. But like any tool, its value depends on what you do with it.

So let's talk about what you're building.

Let's talk about purpose. Freedom. And how to use the systems you've created in this book to design a life that's not just rich in dollars—but rich in meaning.

What Wealth Really Means

As an engineer, you've likely built some amazing things—products, systems, structures, bridges, innovations. But the most complex, high-stakes, customizable thing you'll ever build is your life.

Financial independence isn't just a number. It's a mindset.

It's the ability to walk away from a toxic job without fear.

It's having the space to say no to things that don't serve your mission.

It's the power to support people, ideas, and causes you care about.

It's knowing you could retire tomorrow—but also knowing you don't have to.

This kind of freedom isn't given. It's engineered. Slowly, strategically, persistently.

And every choice you've made up to this point—automating investments, understanding taxes, optimizing your income, protecting your family—has been part of that engineering process.

But the real question is: What are you building that's bigger than you?

The Shift From Security to Significance

Most people spend their early years trying to build security: a stable job, enough in savings to handle emergencies, a roof over their heads.

But once you hit a certain level—once your bills are paid, your investments are humming along, and your income exceeds your lifestyle—it's time to pivot.

You move from security to significance.

Significance means:

- You're no longer only focused on accumulation.
- You're thinking about contribution.
- You're thinking about legacy.
- You're asking, "What impact will I leave?"

This doesn't mean you have to donate millions or start a foundation (unless you want to).

It might mean:

- Teaching your kids to manage money so they don't have to unlearn bad habits.
- Mentoring junior engineers or young professionals just starting their journey.
- Building a scholarship at your alma mater.
- Taking a sabbatical to work on a passion project.

- Being fully present for the people in your life—because your financial systems give you that space.

Freedom gives you time. Purpose gives that time meaning.

Engineer-Led Philanthropy: Giving With Intention

If you've read Chapter 46 on philanthropy, you know that engineers bring something powerful to the world of giving: logic, structure, efficiency.

Whether you're donating to a cause, volunteering your skills, or creating something new entirely, approach it with the same rigor you'd apply to an engineering problem.

Ask:

- What's the outcome I want to create?
- How can I measure impact?
- What are the leverage points?
- Who else is working on this?
- Where can I make the biggest difference?

You don't have to solve everything.

But you do have the ability to solve something.

That's the engineer's advantage: you see systems. You understand scale. You don't waste energy where there's no traction.

Use that mindset. Point it toward what matters most.

From Career Identity to Life Identity

This might be the hardest transition of all.

For decades, you may have introduced yourself by your title:

"I'm a mechanical engineer at Boeing."

"I'm a software developer at a startup."

"I manage systems for a regional utility."

But at some point, your job will end. Your work won't.

Who are you without your business card?

What will fill your days when the meetings, projects, and deadlines disappear?

Too many engineers struggle with this. Not because they didn't save enough money—but because they didn't build a life outside of work.

Start now:

- Explore interests that aren't monetized.
- Cultivate relationships not based on your job.
- Think about what you want your calendar to look like when every day is Saturday.

Because in the end, the goal isn't just to retire from something. It's to retire *to* something.

Your Financial System Is a Living Model

You've built something powerful.

But like any system, your financial life needs maintenance.

You wouldn't design a bridge and walk away from it for 30 years. You'd test it. Calibrate it. Inspect it. Update it for changing conditions.

Do the same with your money:

- Revisit your goals annually.
- Review your investments quarterly.
- Adjust for tax law changes.
- Update your estate plan after major life events.
- Keep learning.

The engineers who win financially aren't the ones who guess.

They're the ones who model, monitor, and improve.

They build feedback loops into their lives.

So set a reminder to revisit your plan.

Create a checklist for your financial spring cleaning.

And never assume the system is finished. It's always under revision.

Final Words From One Engineer to Another

You are more capable than you think.

You don't need a finance degree to master your money. You need the same mindset you already use every day:

- Problem-solving
- Pattern recognition
- Logical frameworks
- Iterative improvements

Financial success isn't about perfection. It's about direction.

You've read 50 chapters.

That's more than most MBAs.

You've equipped yourself with tools that most Americans never get.

You're ready.

Now go engineer something beautiful.

Go build wealth—but more importantly, build a life.

A life where money serves *you*.

Where your values guide your spending.

Where your future isn't left to chance.

This is your blueprint.

Now make it your legacy.

Keep Iterating. Keep Improving. Keep Going.

Because you're not just building a portfolio.

You're building a life of wealth, purpose, and freedom.

And that, engineer, is the most important project of all.

Questions for Professionals

Questions to Ask a Financial Advisor (For Engineers)

- Are you a fiduciary 100% of the time?
- *(Fiduciaries are legally obligated to act in your best interest—no hidden agendas.)*
- Do you work with engineers or other technical professionals with similar income and benefit structures?
- How do you get paid?
- *(Fee-only, fee-based, or commission? Be clear on whether they earn money from selling you products.)*
- Do you help with stock options, RSUs, deferred comp, and equity compensation planning?
- Will you coordinate with my CPA, estate attorney, and other professionals to ensure a cohesive plan?
- What is your investment philosophy?
- *(Ask for simple, jargon-free answers grounded in evidence—not hype.)*
- How do you help clients manage risk and protect assets across life, health, disability, and liability?
- Can you help with real estate investment decisions, rental analysis, or mortgage strategies?
- Are you familiar with FIRE (Financial Independence, Retire Early) principles or early retirement planning?
- Do you provide financial modeling or forecasting tools to simulate outcomes based on engineering-style logic?

Questions to Ask a CPA (Certified Public Accountant)

- Do you work with engineers or self-employed technical consultants?
- Do you offer proactive tax planning throughout the year—or just file returns?
- Are you experienced in handling multi-state income, freelance/contractor work, or RSU/ISO/NSO taxation?
- How do you help high-income earners manage deductions, capital gains, and charitable giving strategies?
- Can you advise on tax-efficient retirement savings (e.g., Roth conversions, backdoor Roths, HSA stacking)?
- Do you assist with tax implications of equity compensation or business ownership?
- Can you help optimize tax planning for real estate investments or rental income?
- Do you provide audit defense or representation if I'm audited by the IRS?

Questions to Ask an Estate Planning Attorney

- Do you specialize in estate plans for high-net-worth individuals or professionals with technical backgrounds?
- What key documents should I have in place?
- *(Will, living trust, durable power of attorney, healthcare directive, etc.)*
- Can you help protect assets from lawsuits, creditors, or future legal disputes?
- How do you structure estate plans for engineers with business ownership, patents, or real estate portfolios?
- Should I consider a revocable living trust, and how would it benefit my family?
- Can you help plan for minor children, blended families, or special-needs dependents?
- How often should I update my estate plan, especially as my assets or income grow?
- Are you willing to coordinate directly with my financial planner or tax

professional?

Questions to Ask a Business Attorney (For Engineers Who Own Firms or Side Businesses)

- Do you have experience working with engineers, consultants, or startup founders?
- Can you help form an LLC, S-Corp, or partnership that's optimal for taxes and liability?
- Will you review or negotiate contracts—employment, consulting, licensing, or non-compete clauses?
- What should I know about intellectual property, patents, or licensing my technology?
- Can you help set up succession planning if I want to sell or exit the company in the next 5–10 years?
- How do you support liability protection or asset shielding strategies?
- Do you charge hourly, by project, or on retainer?

Bonus: Questions to Ask Other Professionals

Insurance Agent (Disability, Life, Umbrella, Liability)

- Are you independent or tied to specific companies?
- Can you explain disability insurance in a way that fits my profession and income risk?
- Do I need an umbrella policy given my income, home equity, or investment assets?
- Can you audit my current insurance policies for gaps or overlaps?
- Do you recommend term or permanent life insurance—and why?

Real Estate Advisor or Investment Property Specialist

- Can you evaluate potential rental properties using engineering-style cash flow models?

- What markets or properties match my investment goals?
- How do you calculate cap rate, cash-on-cash return, and tax implications?

Engineering Career Coach or Consultant

- Can you help me structure an exit strategy if I want to retire early or pivot careers?
- How do you support engineers navigating burnout or planning a 5–10 year transition?
- Can you help quantify the financial impact of grad school, certifications, or career breaks?

Disclaimer

Financial Literacy For Engineers is written with the intent to educate, empower, and encourage engineers at all stages of their careers to take control of their financial lives. The insights in this book are based on the author's personal experience, professional training, and over two decades of work in financial services, engineering education, and personal development.

That said, it's important to be clear on what this book is—and what it is not.

Educational Purpose Only

All content in this book is presented for general educational and informational purposes. It is designed to provide engineers—whether just entering the workforce, climbing the corporate ladder, transitioning to self-employment, or approaching retirement—with essential financial concepts, strategic tools, and awareness of the common opportunities and pitfalls in a high-skill, high-responsibility career.

While this book shares strategies, case studies, and real-world examples, it is not personalized advice, nor should it be used as a substitute for professional consultation. Every engineer's financial situation is unique. Your goals, income level, compensation structure (salary, bonus, stock), family obligations, tax bracket, and risk tolerance must be taken into account.

Before making any major financial, legal, or business decisions, you should work with licensed professionals who understand your specific needs.

No Legal Advice

Although many engineers eventually deal with contracts, IP agreements, consulting projects, or even business ownership, this book does not provide legal advice. It is not a replacement for working with a qualified attorney.

If you are:

- Signing or renegotiating an employment or consulting contract
- Structuring a business entity or startup
- Protecting intellectual property or licensing technology
- Navigating liability risk or non-compete clauses
- Creating estate planning documents

...you should seek the advice of an attorney who specializes in employment law, contract law, intellectual property, or estate planning. Legal requirements vary by state, country, and industry. You are responsible for understanding and complying with all applicable regulations and agreements.

No Financial or Investment Advice

This book discusses important topics like budgeting, equity compensation, investing, taxes, retirement planning, and long-term wealth-building—but from an educational standpoint, not an advisory one.

This book is not written by a Certified Financial Planner™, Registered Investment Advisor, or broker-dealer. The examples and frameworks shared are general in nature and may not apply directly to your specific circumstances.

Before implementing any financial strategy, investing in any product, or making significant decisions about your money, consult a licensed financial professional—preferably one experienced in working with engineers or other high-income technical professionals.

Your 401(k), RSUs, deferred compensation plan, or company stock options are too important to leave to guesswork.

No Accounting or Tax Advice

Taxes are an integral part of wealth-building, especially for high-earning engineers with complex compensation packages. However, this book is not written by a CPA, enrolled agent, or tax preparer. Any references to deductions, tax brackets, or IRS rules are intended for general awareness only.

If you:

- Work as a contractor or run a side hustle
- Hold equity in a startup or company stock
- Earn income from multiple states or countries
- Contribute to multiple retirement accounts
- Want to explore tax-loss harvesting, Roth conversions, or advanced tax strategies

...you should hire a qualified tax advisor or CPA. Only a licensed tax professional can review your situation, determine what applies, and guide you through proper compliance while optimizing your tax outcomes.

No Guarantees or Promises

Reading this book does not guarantee financial success, investment returns, early retirement, or any specific outcome. Financial literacy is not a one-time lesson—it's an ongoing process that requires attention, discipline, and adaptability.

Any examples, case studies, or illustrations included in this book are for demonstration purposes only. They are not a promise or prediction. Outcomes will always depend on your decisions, behaviors, life circumstances, and market conditions.

Limitation of Liability

By reading this book, you agree that the author, Pat Brown, MBA, and all affiliated websites and brands—such as FinancialLiteracyForEngineers.com, FinancialLiteracyForNIL.com, and others—are not responsible for your financial outcomes, legal disputes, or tax consequences.

Neither the author nor any associated entity shall be held liable for any financial losses, legal claims, tax liabilities, or negative results related to your use of the information in this book. You are fully responsible for your financial decisions.

Encouragement to Build Your Team

It is the author's sincere belief that every engineer—whether in aerospace, software, electrical, civil, or systems engineering—deserves a reliable team of professionals: a financial planner, tax advisor, attorney, and insurance specialist.

This book is meant to **complement** that team—not replace it.

If you haven't assembled your team yet, now is the time. Financial systems don't build themselves. But you, as an engineer, already understand the power of planning, systems, precision, and continuous improvement. Your money deserves the same level of intentionality as your career.

You've spent years solving problems, leading projects, and building a future for your company or clients.

Now it's time to make sure you engineer a financial life that works just as efficiently—for you.

Annual Financial Calendar – Important Dates Every Engineer Should Know

JANUARY

January 1

- New contribution limits for 401(k), 403(b), 457, and IRA/Roth IRA go into effect.
- Health Savings Account (HSA) and Flexible Spending Account (FSA) limits reset.
- Begin new year's budget and cash flow review.
- Update paycheck withholding (Form W-4) if you've had life changes.

January 15

- 4th Quarter Estimated Taxes Due (for income earned October 1 – December 31 of previous year). Use IRS Form 1040-ES.

Late January

- Begin receiving W-2s, 1099-NEC, 1099-MISC, 1099-INT, 1099-DIV, and 1099-B from employers, banks, brokerages, and clients.

FEBRUARY

February 1

- Deadline for employers and payers to issue W-2s and 1099s to employees and contractors.

Mid to Late February

- Receive K-1s from partnerships or S-corporations (may be delayed into March or April).
- Start preparing documentation for tax filing or submission to your CPA.

MARCH

March 15

- Partnership and S-Corporation Tax Returns Due (Form 1065 or 1120-S).
- Can file extension using Form 7004.

March 31

- Last day to receive electronic Form 1095-A, 1095-B, or 1095-C (health insurance coverage documentation).

APRIL

April 1

- Required Minimum Distributions (RMDs) must begin if you turned 73 last year and delayed your first RMD.

April 15 (or next business day if weekend/holiday)

- Personal Tax Filing Deadline (Form 1040)
- First Quarter Estimated Taxes Due
- Deadline to make prior-year contributions to:
- Traditional IRA / Roth IRA

- SEP IRA
- HSA
- Coverdell Education Savings Account (ESA)
- Last day to file for a 6-month tax extension (Form 4868).
- Last day to file FAFSA in some states if applying for financial aid (for dependent children).

MAY

Early May

- Review property tax assessments if applicable. Protest deadline usually mid-May depending on your state.

May 29 (5/29)

- National 529 College Savings Plan Day – Great reminder to review or open 529 accounts for children.

JUNE

June 15

- 2nd Quarter Estimated Taxes Due
- U.S. Citizens Abroad tax filing deadline (can extend to October 15).

Mid-June

- Mid-year retirement account performance review. Adjust contributions if needed.
- Reassess charitable giving plans for the year.

JULY

July 1–15

- Mid-year financial check-in:
- Review spending, savings goals, debt paydown progress.
- Rebalance portfolio if allocation is off by more than 5–10%.
- Schedule a meeting with your financial advisor or CPA.

AUGUST

August 1–31

- Plan for open enrollment (usually starts in October or November).
- Review HSA/FSA balances and projected usage.
- Review insurance policies: life, disability, malpractice, and umbrella coverage.
- Prep for year-end charitable planning (DAFs, appreciated stock, QCDs if age 70½+).

SEPTEMBER

September 15

- 3rd Quarter Estimated Taxes Due
- Tax Deadline for Calendar-Year Partnerships and S-Corps (if on extension)

Late September

- Check for any backdoor Roth IRA contributions to convert before year-end.
- Consider harvesting capital losses to offset gains before Q4 ends.

OCTOBER

October 1

- Deadline for establishing a SIMPLE IRA for current tax year.
- Medicare Open Enrollment preview window begins (important for

you, parents, or retired patients).

October 15

- Extended Individual Tax Return Due Date (Form 1040 with extension).
- Deadline to fund SEP IRA for prior year (if filed extension).
- Deadline to recharacterize prior-year Roth IRA contributions.

Late October

- Review open enrollment options for employer-sponsored insurance.

NOVEMBER

November 1–30

- Health Insurance Open Enrollment begins for ACA Marketplace.
- Employer benefits enrollment usually begins. Reassess:
- Health plans (HSA-eligible?)
- Life & disability insurance
- 401(k) contribution changes
- FSA/HSA elections
- Legal services or supplemental benefits

Black Friday Weekend

- Consider timing large purchases with end-of-year spending and cash flow planning.

DECEMBER

December 1–15

- Last call to max out retirement accounts:
- 401(k), 403(b), 457 contributions

- HSA contributions (if payroll deductions)
- Backdoor Roth conversion

December 31

- Last day for:
- Charitable contributions to count for current year (check DAF cutoffs).
- Tax-loss harvesting (sell losers to offset capital gains).
- RMDs for age 73+ (Required Minimum Distributions).
- Gifting up to $18,000 per recipient (annual exclusion for gift tax).
- Spend down FSA funds (check for grace period or carryover).
- Convert to Roth IRA (backdoor Roth deadline).
- Complete year-end bonuses and profit-sharing contributions for S-corps.

BONUS: Rolling & Event-Based Reminders
Every Paycheck:

- Check 401(k)/403(b) deductions.
- Verify health/dental/vision premiums and HSA contributions.

After Major Life Events:

- Marriage/divorce
- Birth/adoption of child
- New job or contract
- Disability or injury
- Change of primary residence
- Significant windfall/inheritance

Quarterly:

- Revisit budget and spending.

- Make estimated tax payments if self-employed or have side income.
- Review investment performance and allocations.
- Meet with advisor if pursuing tax-loss harvesting or Roth conversions.

Final Tip: Automate What You Can

- Set calendar reminders.
- Automate contributions.
- Set up recurring transfers.

The less reliant you are on memory, the more consistent your wealth-building habits will become.

Financial Literacy Resources for Engineers

1. **Financial Literacy for Engineers**
2. A dedicated platform offering practical guides, tools, and educational resources tailored to the financial lives of engineers at every career stage.
3. **The Engineer's Guide to Financial Mastery**
4. An insightful article providing strategies for engineers to achieve financial independence, covering topics like budgeting, investing, and retirement planning.
5. **ARQ Wealth Advisors – Financial Planning Tips for Engineers**
6. Offers expert advice on maximizing 401(k) and HSA contributions, increasing earnings, and building a solid financial foundation.
7. **Personal Finance for Engineers – Engineering.com**
8. A comprehensive guide discussing key financial principles, including asset management, tax strategies, and wealth-building techniques.
9. **Financial Acumen for Engineers – Engineering Education Australia**
10. A course aimed at enhancing engineers' financial decision-making skills, focusing on budgeting, financial reporting, and investment analysis.
11. **Financial Literacy for Engineering Graduates – OTM Online**
12. Provides budgeting tools and resources to help new engineering graduates manage expenses and plan for financial goals.
13. **The Engineer's Guide to Financial Planning – Lakewood Wealth**

14. Discusses building wealth with precision, emphasizing goal setting, data analysis, and diversified investments.
15. **Financial Planning Challenges for Engineers – Bollin Wealth Management**
16. Highlights common financial hurdles engineers face, such as tax management and career volatility, offering solutions to overcome them.
17. **Financial Literacy for Engineers – MRS Fall Meeting & Exhibit**
18. A presentation introducing fundamental financial concepts tailored to science and engineering students.
19. **Financial Literacy Modules for Engineers – University of Iowa**
20. Educational modules covering concepts like interest, present value, and depreciation, integrating engineering and business principles.
21. **WorldQuant University – MSc in Financial Engineering**
22. Offers a free, accredited online master's program focusing on quantitative finance, ideal for engineers interested in financial markets.
23. **Corporate Finance Institute (CFI)**
24. Provides online courses and certifications in financial modeling, valuation, and corporate finance, suitable for engineers seeking to enhance financial skills.
25. **Investopedia – Financial Literacy Resources**
26. A comprehensive platform offering tutorials, articles, and tools to improve financial knowledge across various topics.
27. **Wall Street Survivor**
28. An educational website using gamification to teach investing and personal finance concepts, allowing engineers to practice with virtual portfolios.
29. **Next Gen Personal Finance (NGPF)**
30. Offers free courses and resources in personal finance, beneficial for engineers looking to strengthen their financial literacy.
31. **Federal Reserve Education**
32. Provides educational materials on economics and personal finance, helping engineers understand broader financial systems.

33. **Financial Literacy and the Engineer – YouTube Webinar**
34. A webinar introducing basic financial concepts tailored for engineers, covering topics like budgeting, saving, and investing.
35. **Refactoring – Personal Finance for Engineers**
36. An article discussing the importance of financial planning for engineers, offering practical advice on managing finances effectively.
37. **Engineering Financial Literacy – Stanford d.school**
38. Highlights initiatives aimed at improving financial literacy among engineers through design thinking and innovative approaches.
39. **Financial Planning for Engineers – Scripted.com**
40. A guide outlining steps for engineers to create effective financial plans, emphasizing the importance of budgeting and goal setting.

These resources are designed to empower engineers with the knowledge and tools necessary to make informed financial decisions throughout their careers.

About The Author

Patrick Brown, MBA, is a former Division I football player turned wealth advisor, educator, and nationally respected voice in financial literacy. With more than two decades of experience in financial planning, insurance, and investment strategy, Patrick has made it his mission to help individuals and families build wealth with clarity, confidence, and long-term vision.

After earning his MBA and launching a successful career in wealth management, Patrick created a series of financial literacy platforms aimed at educating overlooked and underserved communities. These include:

- Financial Literacy For NIL
- Financial Literacy For Student Athletes
- Financial Literacy For The Culture
- Financial Literacy For College Coaches
- Parents Of Student Athletes

Now, through *Financial Literacy For Engineers,* Patrick brings his mission to one of the most analytically minded professions in the world. Engineers are known for solving complex problems, designing systems, and building structures—but many have never been taught how to apply that same precision to their personal finances. Patrick's goal is to change that.

His passion for financial education is rooted in personal experience. Raised in a home where money was rarely discussed, he saw firsthand how financial insecurity and silence around money matters could derail promising futures. He's committed to bridging the gap between earning income and building sustainable, generational wealth.

Patrick has become a trusted advisor to a diverse range of clients—

including engineers, physicians, student-athletes, retirees, and young professionals. His approach is practical, culturally aware, and grounded in real-life scenarios—not jargon. Whether you're a recent engineering graduate just starting out or a seasoned technical leader planning retirement, Patrick's advice is designed to meet you where you are and help you move forward—strategically.

Outside of his financial work, Patrick is deeply involved in community leadership. He serves as a Trustee on the Board of Lawrence Memorial Hospital (LMH) and participates in hospital board committees focused on governance, strategic planning, and patient outcomes. He also serves on several nonprofit and civic boards across the region, advocating for financial literacy, family support, and healthcare access.

Above all, Patrick is a proud husband and father. When he's not helping others navigate their financial lives, he enjoys speaking at engineering schools, community events, and professional organizations—translating financial education into stories that stick and strategies that work.

He believes financial literacy is about more than money—it's about options, freedom, and designing a life you're proud to live.

Final Word

Need Help? Start Here

This book exists because financial education is a powerful tool. When used well, it can open doors, protect your legacy, and give you the confidence to take control of your future.

But just like engineering, the game isn't won with guesswork. You need structure. You need systems. You need the ability to ask the right questions, evaluate trade-offs, and know when to bring in specialists. It's not about mastering every detail—it's about knowing how to navigate decisions with clarity and confidence.

Use this book as a guide—not a rule book. Let it inspire action. Let it help you build momentum. But don't treat it as a substitute for professional advice. Be curious. Stay informed. Keep asking good questions before making any major financial decisions.

Trusted Resources

If you're looking for guidance or just want to talk through next steps, reach out to professionals who understand your world—engineering, systems thinking, and the pressure of real-world decision-making.

Pat Brown, MBA

Former D1 athlete. Wealth advisor. Financial literacy advocate.

Advisor to engineers, student-athletes, and high-performing professionals nationwide.

- Website: www.financialliteracyfornil.com
- Email: info@financialliteracyfornil.com

Join Our Newsletter

Stay updated with insights, resources, and reminders that help you stay financially sharp—delivered directly to your inbox.

Final Word: Use This. Don't Shelf It.

These tools aren't meant to collect dust in a drawer or sit unread in the back of a binder. Use them. Revisit them. Share them with someone who needs them. Apply what works, test what doesn't, and keep refining your process.

This is your playbook for life—professionally, personally, and financially.

Stay sharp. Stay curious. Keep engineering a better future.

Pros and Cons of Working with a Financial Advisor

Working with a Financial Advisor: Is It the Right Move for an Engineer?

As an engineer, you're trained to solve complex problems, manage detailed systems, and make data-driven decisions. But when it comes to your own finances, you may wonder whether it makes sense to do it all yourself—or hire a professional to help manage the big picture.

The reality? Working with a financial advisor can offer tremendous value, especially for engineers with demanding jobs, high income, or complex financial goals. But just like any engineering project, it's important to weigh the pros and cons before committing.

Pros of Working with a Financial Advisor

1. Cross-Disciplinary Expertise

A qualified financial advisor brings broad expertise in investing, tax strategy, risk management, insurance, estate planning, and retirement modeling. For engineers with stock compensation, side ventures, or business aspirations, this comprehensive view can be crucial to long-term success.

2. Time-Saving and Stress-Reducing

You already spend your day troubleshooting, leading teams, or optimizing workflows. Researching Roth conversion strategies, reviewing long-term care coverage, or analyzing tax bracket impacts might not be at the top of your list when you get home. Delegating this to a trusted advisor saves time, reduces stress, and frees up bandwidth for the parts of life you care about most.

3. Rational, Objective Guidance

Even logical thinkers like engineers are human. Market volatility, sudden windfalls, or family pressure can lead to reactive decisions. An advisor acts as a buffer between your emotions and your money—helping you zoom out, stay calm, and think long-term when markets or life get turbulent.

4. Accountability and Follow-Through

Engineers love systems—but building financial systems takes work. An advisor helps make sure the important (but easy to postpone) tasks—updating beneficiaries, rebalancing accounts, purchasing umbrella insurance—actually get done. They become your implementation partner, not just your planner.

5. Customized Planning That Fits You

A solid financial advisor doesn't hand you a templated plan—they ask about your priorities, career path, company benefits, RSUs, and long-term vision. Whether you're an early-career software engineer climbing the ladder or a late-career engineer preparing to exit your business, the advice is tailored to your numbers *and* your values.

Cons of Working with a Financial Advisor

1. The Cost

Advisors charge fees—often a percentage of assets (typically 0.5% to 1%), a flat fee, or hourly rates. For younger engineers just starting to invest, the fees may feel like a hurdle. It's important to understand what services you're getting in return—and whether they justify the price tag.

2. Quality and Transparency Aren't Universal

Not all advisors are created equal. Some are fiduciaries legally required to act in your best interest; others are brokers or insurance reps selling commission-based products. You need to do your due diligence—ask the tough questions, and understand how they're compensated.

3. It's Not "Set It and Forget It"

Even with a great advisor, you can't completely disengage. You'll still need to participate in big decisions—especially around risk tolerance, legacy planning, job transitions, and lifestyle shifts. Advisors can steer the ship, but you're still the captain.

4. Risk of Generic, Templated Advice

Some advisors rely on canned portfolios or one-size-fits-all plans. If they're not asking detailed questions about your specific income structure, employer stock plans, side income, or values, they may not be the right fit. Engineers expect precision—your financial advice should be no different.

5. You Might Not Need One—Yet

If you're financially literate, enjoy managing your own investments, and have relatively simple needs (e.g., contributing to a 401(k), no dependents, low debt), then DIY might work. Low-cost platforms, automation tools, and index funds have made it easier than ever to build a solid financial foundation on your own.

So... Should You Hire a Financial Advisor?

Ask yourself these questions:

- Do I have the time, tools, and discipline to manage my finances consistently?
- Am I confident in my investment, tax, and protection strategies?
- Do I feel overwhelmed or stuck when trying to prioritize financial decisions?
- Am I making full use of my employer benefits, equity comp, and tax planning tools?
- Would having a guide increase my peace of mind and help me avoid costly errors?

If you answered "no" to one or more of these, an advisor might be worth considering. The best ones don't just manage money—they educate, strategize, and help you align your financial plan with the life you want to build.

Made in United States
Orlando, FL
04 November 2026

90201050R00223